Early Praise for *Guiding Star OKRs*

Guiding Star OKRs creatively reimagines the OKR framework, transforming it from a tactical performance management tool into a compass for cultivating a culture of learning, adapting, and strategic navigation of today's complex business landscape. Complex concepts are brilliantly simplified in a way that readers of all experience levels will find engaging and useful.

➤ **Darren Gandy**
   VP, Agile Portfolio Management

This book provides a hands-on approach for how to drive a company using strategic objectives. Its unique approach shows you how to do this while at the same time maintaining adaptability as well as autonomy and engagement among all employees. Highly recommended!

➤ **Henrik Berglund**
   Agile Leadership Coach

Staffan's *Guiding Star OKRs* brings OKRs to life with clear, practical guidance that makes the whole process accessible and enjoyable This book goes beyond theory—Staffan's fresh approach takes us from high-level strategy down to actionable steps, blending big-picture direction with everyday execution. The collaborative methods, like catchball and cross-pollination, make OKRs a team effort where every perspective counts. I really like the relatable examples and straightforward instructions!

➤ **Sandy Mamoli**
   Coauthor of *Creating Great Teams: How Self-Selection Lets People Excel*

During my first years as an Agile coach, most of my attention was on the team level, helping teams improve their internal collaboration and way of working. Nowadays, this is seldom an issue, but aligning many teams toward a common and clear direction is still a big issue. So much potential is lost due to having teams running unaligned and without any supporting structure and process to help everybody assess the ROI. Staffan is giving us a pragmatic set of principles and tools to address this gap, in his usual entertaining way of writing. I highly recommend this book to use as a guide in improving your strategy process.

➤ **Anders Laestadius**
   Enterprise Agile Coach

Guiding Star OKRs provides a comprehensive framework for starting, refining, and anchoring OKRs within your organization.

➤ **Bjørn-Henrik Zink**
   Engineering Lead

The Guiding Star OKRs framework offers a powerful approach to crafting flexible, adaptive strategies that guide organizations through complexity. By setting clear objectives that provide direction while allowing for adaptability, the framework empowers individuals and teams to engage, innovate, and take ownership of the organization's strategy. This book is a practical, easy-to-read guide packed with hands-on instructions, examples, and versatile tools that bring the concept to life. It's a must-read for anyone looking to master goal setting and strategic planning in today's business landscape. Highly recommended.

➤ **Tommy Ågren**
   Senior Agile Coach

With *Guiding Star OKRs*, I have found a way to integrate strategy with our development efforts without getting just another framework that governs our business.

➤ **Magnus Lindberg**
    Chief Development Officer

Setting, tracking, and reporting OKRs is terrible. But what if it wasn't? In *Guiding Star OKRs*, Staffan Nöteberg lays out a framework that focuses on heading in the right direction instead of trying to meet exact targets. This book is full of practical advice and examples to help the reader adopt the framework to their organization's specific needs. Guiding Star OKRs is a must-read for leaders who want to achieve results in a sustainable way.

➤ **Ben Cotton**
    Author of *Program Management for Open Source Projects*

Guiding Star OKRs

A New Approach to Setting and Achieving Goals

Staffan Nöteberg

The Pragmatic Bookshelf

Dallas, Texas

See our complete catalog of hands-on, practical,
and Pragmatic content for software developers:
https://pragprog.com

Sales, volume licensing, and support:
support@pragprog.com

Derivative works, AI training and testing,
international translations, and other rights:
rights@pragprog.com

The team that produced this book includes:

Publisher: Dave Thomas
COO: Janet Furlow
Executive Editor: Susannah Davidson
Development Editor: Katharine Dvorak
Copy Editor: Corina Lebegioara
Indexing: Potomac Indexing, LLC
Layout: Gilson Graphics

ISBN-13: 979-8-88865-128-5
Book version: P1.0—March 2025

Contents

Part II — Guiding Stars in Action

Part III — Succeeding with Guiding Stars

Acknowledgments

I am grateful to my beta readers for their thoughtful comments and suggestions: Anders Jönsson, Anders Laestadius, Anni Nöteberg, Bjørn-Henrik Zink, Carl Nordenfelt, Darren Gandy, Erik Schön, Henrik Berglund, Jonathan Rasmusson, Magnus Lindberg, Magnus Olofsson, Peter Krantz, Petra Karmteg, Sandy Mamoli, Tommy Ågren, and Viktor Cessan.

Thank you to the anecdote contributors: Joakim Manding Holm, Martin Christensen, and Ola Ellnestam.

A special thank you to my editor, Katharine Dvorak, for her guidance and feedback.

Introduction: The Strategy Challenge

Imagine your company is holding a conference in a new city. As you explore, you discover various vantage points offering unique perspectives of the city-scape. From one, you might spot the towering church steeple, while another reveals the grand city hall, and yet another showcases the sprawling sports arena. Each viewpoint provides a glimpse of the city's essence, but none captures its entirety.

The same principle applies in a corporate setting. Let's say you're seeing things from the "Project Management" viewpoint. From here, you clearly see the projects, timelines, and budgets. Your job is to ensure timely and on-budget delivery while meeting all requirements. You focus on the company fulfilling its commitments.

By shifting your focus to the "Agile Coaching" viewpoint, you gain insights into the teams themselves—their drive, their collaboration, and their overall dynamic. Here, your role is to empower them, ensuring they're both productive and comfortable taking risks. Ultimately, you want to foster a sense of ownership and autonomy within each team.

From the "Product Management" viewpoint, you see the customers and their needs. You see how the company's products are used and what problems they solve. Your job is to ensure that the products are user-friendly and to take care of customer problems.

From the "Chief Technology Officer" viewpoint, you see the technical infrastructure and the need for standardization. You propose a new process to coordinate development, reduce costs, and increase clarity. Your goal is to optimize resource utilization.

But many more viewpoints exist. Take, for example, "Software Development," where the technical debt is seen, or "Sales," where the extra feature that enables big deals is clearly visible. "HR," "Testing," "Marketing"—there are almost as many viewpoints as there are employees in the company. Everyone in the company, regardless of their viewpoint, wants the company to be successful. They just have very different ideas about how best to get there.

But, wait a minute! Shouldn't there be a viewpoint marked "Strategy"? A place everyone in the company visits now and again? From there, they can see the company's long-term goals and how they fit into the larger market. They can see the threats and opportunities that exist and how the company can position itself for success. This viewpoint offers a collective understanding of the company's future vision, and everyone knows that this understanding is shared by all. This "Strategy" viewpoint is—unfortunately—a whole different ball game compared to the others.

Balancing the Trifecta of Strategic Execution

Alignment—the ability to ensure everyone works together in the same direction, even when coming from different viewpoints—is the first of three key challenges that this book addresses. The second challenge is persistence—the unwavering commitment to progress in that direction, regardless of obstacles. The third is adaptability—the capacity to continuously adjust and refine your approach based on new information and a changing landscape.

Throughout this book, we'll revisit the powerful combination of alignment, persistence, and adaptability. To help you remember them, think of a field of sunflowers, a beaver colony, and a flowing river.

- *Alignment*: Each sunflower in a large field has its own place and role, but they all strive to face the same star—the sun. The sunflower bud follows the sun's movement during the day from east to west. No one gives orders, yet they're aligned.

- *Persistence*: A beaver colony can patiently work for weeks or months to build a dam, and then the colony maintains and strengthens this structure for years. The largest dams can be 100 meters wide!

- *Adaptability*: The river constantly changes its course to navigate around obstacles and follow the path of least resistance. Changes in the environment cause it to reorganize, but the river still strives toward the same lake or sea.

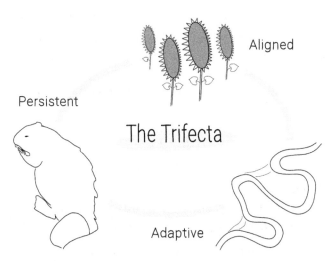

You can likely think of companies that embody one or two of these characteristics, but the true challenge lies in achieving all three—persistence, alignment, and adaptability—simultaneously in pursuit of long-term goals. This is the trifecta challenge: to balance these forces without stifling any of them.

The desire to achieve this trifecta balance isn't unique to your company. Many organizations struggle to do so. That's where guiding star OKRs come in, and why you might find this book valuable.

Why You Might Find This Book Valuable

Perhaps you picked up this book because you're a curious leader wondering if OKR—objectives and key results—might be the right tool to help your team achieve its goals. You might hope to learn how to create OKRs that are both ambitious and realistic and how to get the whole team on board.

Or maybe you work in a development team and have heard about OKR as a way to increase focus and collaboration. You're curious about how OKRs can help you deliver the right software without micromanagement from your managers.

Or you might be an experienced consultant who has used OKRs before, and you want to deepen your understanding of the framework. You might be looking for new ideas and inspiration to help your clients make their OKRs more effective.

You might also be a leadership coach who wants to learn more about modern leadership methods. You're curious about how OKRs can help organizations become more agile and adaptable in an ever-changing world.

No matter who you're, I hope this book will be both interesting and inspiring. It might be helpful to know that all examples are drawn from real-world experiences, although some names and industries have been changed to maintain confidentiality. These courageous organizations not only recognized recurring mistakes but also dared to experiment with new, more modern ways of working together toward long-term goals.

A New Approach to Strategy

The book's theme—guiding stars—is a new approach to the decades-old OKR framework. Back in the 1970s, Intel's CEO, Andy Grove, developed a system called iMBOs (Intel Management by Objectives), likely influenced by Peter Drucker's seminal 1954 book, *The Practice of Management [Dru54]*.

John Doerr, a venture capitalist who worked at Intel under Grove, brought the iMBO concept to the venture capital firm Kleiner Perkins. Then, in 1999, Doerr introduced the OKR concept to a young company called Google, where it was a success. Google's founders, Larry Page and Sergey Brin, embraced the OKR framework and adapted it to their own company culture.

With Google's buy-in, the OKR framework spread to LinkedIn, Twitter, Uber, and other tech companies in Silicon Valley. But the practice didn't stop there. There are case studies on how Samsung, Spotify, government agencies, non-profits, and many others use OKRs.

Now, you might be wondering, "How exactly does this Guiding Star approach differ from the OKRs I've encountered before?" And you're right to ask. The truth is that many organizations find themselves trapped in a cycle of setting ambitious goals but struggling to achieve them. Often, this is due to a focus on measuring performance rather than fostering a culture of continuous observing, orienting, and calibrating. For example, John Doerr writes in *Measure What Matters [Doe18]*: "A committed OKR that fails to achieve a 1.0 by its due date requires a postmortem." Regardless of Doerr's intentions, being required to write the postmortem can make an employee feel solely responsible for the failure of an OKR, fostering a culture of shame that discourages risk-taking and innovation.

The following image illustrates two different approaches to goal-setting. Traditionally, you start a quarter by planning tasks (diamond point) and then selecting one as a challenging goal (open circle). But this goal often ends up disconnected from daily work until the end of the quarter when you check if you achieved it (filled circle). This "set-and-check" or even "set-and-forget" method doesn't make the goal more likely to happen.

The Guiding Star paradigm is different. Guiding stars establish a clear direction well before planning the quarter (green bar) and then influence both your planning and the teams' daily work, promoting a proactive approach that the traditional method simply cannot achieve.

With the Guiding Star framework, we shift our focus away from punitive grading and toward a more holistic, scalable, and forward-looking approach that empowers teams to learn, adapt, and ultimately achieve more and more meaningful results. This book will guide you through that shift, providing a roadmap for implementing a goal-setting process that truly aligns with the dynamic nature of today's business landscape.

A Map of the Book

Let's take a quick look at what lies ahead. The success of any goal-setting framework hinges on a process that's not only understood but also embraced by everyone in the organization. The Guiding Star OKR framework, while designed to tackle complex challenges in large companies, emphasizes collaboration and encourages the spontaneous interactions that lead to greater alignment, persistence, and adaptability. We'll delve into these collaborative methods in Part II.

Feel free to explore the chapters in any order that speaks to you. To help you get started, I recommend skimming the map of the book, then reading the section that follows, which emphasizes that large-scale collaboration toward a common goal is more natural than you might think, and after that jumping straight into the chapter that sparks your interest.

Part I—Setting the Foundation

The first two of this book's ten chapters comprise Part I, where we delve into the essence of the objectives and key results that serve as guiding stars, their significance, and their distinctions from traditional goal-setting frameworks. You'll discover that checking off isolated tasks isn't enough—you also want a common direction and meaning for the entire organization.

Chapter 1, Guiding Star Objectives, on page 3

This chapter explains how the objective (the "O" in an OKR) can guide the company's transformation and investments in new capabilities for your customers. We will discuss how to formulate effective and qualitative objectives that inspire and focus your team. For instance, have you considered that objectives can signify far more to the organization than merely a scope of work to deliver?

Chapter 2, Guiding Star Key Results, on page 15

Now that you have a handle on the objectives, it's time to set key results (the "KR" in an OKR) that will help you get there. You'll learn how key quantitative results can be the compass that shows the way toward the objective. You might be surprised that key results within the Guiding Star OKR framework aren't about proving that you've reached the objective. Instead, they're about understanding what the objective means.

Part II—Guiding Stars in Action

In Part II, it's time to roll up your sleeves and put theory into practice. Chapter by chapter, you get the concrete tools and methods you need to find, formulate, and work toward guiding stars in your organization. We'll examine how you can create engagement, collaborate effectively, and adapt to changes.

Chapter 3, Discovering Customer Opportunities, on page 29

This chapter is about understanding your customers' real needs and desires, even those they might not have thought of themselves. We'll delve into how to set guiding stars that not only improve your current products but create entirely new capabilities for your customers. By understanding the entire ecosystem around your customers, you can create products and services that exceed their expectations.

Chapter 4, Catchball: Defining Guiding Stars Cross-Collaboratively, on page 41

Here, we discuss the catchball process, a way to set goals that utilize everyone's knowledge and experience. You'll discover how hierarchy and collaboration can go hand in hand, even if you might not be so fond of hierarchies. The focus is on setting goals of different granularities, not on who decides.

Chapter 5, Pupation: Integrating Guiding Stars with Agile Planning, on page 55

In the hustle of daily work, it's easy for urgent tasks to overshadow those important for long-term success. We'll explore how to seamlessly integrate guiding stars, your long-term vision, into your agile planning processes—whether it's sprint planning, quarterly planning, or any other timeboxed approach. You'll discover surprisingly simple yet effective techniques to achieve this balance.

Chapter 6, Calibration: Fine-Tuning Guiding Stars, on page 65

Imagine being able to adjust and improve your goals along the way. That's precisely what calibration is all about. You'll learn how to keep your guiding stars up-to-date and relevant, even when you gain new insights or the world around you changes. Calibration is also a powerful tool for increasing motivation and engagement among your colleagues.

Chapter 7, Cross-Pollination: Everyone's Ears, Insights, and Ideas, on page 79

Unexpected encounters and creative discussions can lead to entirely new insights. How can we further enhance this valuable exchange of information? In this chapter, you'll learn a concrete method to mix different ingredients to create, share, and learn something novel. People are often surprised by how much creativity and innovation can be unleashed when you loosen constraints in a session.

Part III—Succeeding with Guiding Stars

In the final part of this book, we will walk through seven principles based on the key takeaways in the previous parts and offer practical guidance on implementing the Guiding Star OKR framework in your organization. We'll also examine common challenges and how to overcome them, ensuring you're well-prepared to embark on your OKR journey.

Chapter 8, Seven Principles of Good Strategy, on page 95
> Here, we distill the key takeaways from this book into seven fundamental principles for crafting a successful strategy. For example, it's important to remember that having all the answers at the outset isn't always essential. Sometimes, the most effective approach is to embrace new opportunities and adapt as you learn.

Chapter 9, Implementing the Guiding Star OKR Framework, on page 105
> This chapter serves as your hands-on guide to introducing the Guiding Star OKR framework within your organization. You'll find that involving everyone in the implementation process fosters smoother transitions and greater acceptance. We'll also explore the advantages of starting small and allowing the process to evolve organically, rather than attempting a sweeping, immediate overhaul.

Chapter 10, Overcoming Guiding Star Challenges, on page 117
> In this chapter, we'll address common obstacles that organizations face when implementing the Guiding Star OKR framework and offer strategies for overcoming them. We'll draw from real-world examples to provide practical solutions and insights. By understanding these challenges upfront, you'll be better equipped to navigate the complexities of your implementation.

Appendix

Appendix 1, Glossary, on page 131
> Some terms are used in specific ways to fit this book's context. They might have different meanings in other fields. To avoid confusion and make sure we're all on the same page, this glossary aims to clarify how key terms are used in the Guiding Star OKR framework.

The image on page xxi illustrates the iterative flow of guiding star OKRs, highlighting the key steps of catchball, strategy broadcast, pupation, and strategic execution. Discovery of the customers' real needs—while not part of a specific iteration—underpins the entire process. The numbers in the image represent the chapters in Parts I and II of this book.

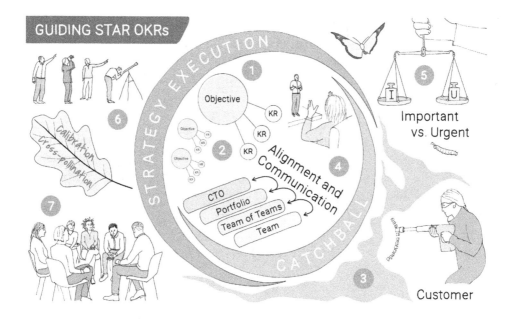

This book has a companion website[1] on pragprog.com. There you'll find a forum for discussion, as well as a place to report any errors you may encounter. If you have any reflections, comments, or questions, please feel free to reach out to me directly at mailto:staffan.noteberg@rekursiv.se. Your feedback is invaluable in helping to make this book the best it can be.

You have an enriching journey ahead of you. The Guiding Star OKR framework is comprehensive, but before you embark, remember that large-scale collaboration toward a shared goal wasn't invented during the Industrial Revolution. It's a fundamental part of nature itself.

Scaling Collaboration Is Natural

You might have heard of the Digesting Duck.[2] It was a sensation in its day. The life-size duck was made of copper, gold, and steel. It could flap its wings, quack, and even appear to eat and digest grain. Its 18th-century French inventor, Jacques de Vaucanson, achieved this by using a complicated system of gears, levers, and springs. But the "digestion" was fake: the grain was stored in a hidden compartment and released at an appropriate time.

---

1.   https://pragprog.com/titles/snokrs/guiding-star-okrs
2.   https://www.aps.org/archives/publications/apsnews/201802/history.cfm

In truth, it's understandable that Jacques de Vaucanson took a shortcut when trying to mimic something as complex as digestion. If you're an average human then you host nearly 40 trillion bacteria.[3] That's, by the way, over 100 times the number of stars in our galaxy.[4] Most of these bacteria live in your gut where they collaborate to break down food, allowing your body to absorb nutrients and convert them into energy.

Your bacteria have no central control mechanism—a boss bacterium micro-managing what each individual bacterium should do. Yet, they spontaneously cooperate to achieve their shared goal of breaking down everything you consume, regardless of the ever-changing variety in your diet.

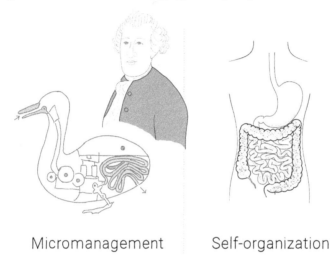

Micromanagement   Self-organization

Micromanagement structures rarely excel in large-scale human collaboration either, especially not in creative endeavors like developing products and services. When many people work together toward evolving goals, countless interactions occur. Some are planned meetings, but most are spontaneous and shaped by previous events. This constant feedback loop adapts everyone's work. Overly centralized control is a bottleneck in this evolving, complex situation, reducing both speed and quality.

No company has 40 trillion employees, but even with 50 people, the potential relationships exceed 1,000. In a large company with 5,000 employees, over 12 million different pairings could collaborate.

---

3.   https://www.nature.com/articles/nature.2016.19136

4.   https://www.esa.int/Science_Exploration/Space_Science/Herschel/How_many_stars_are_there_in_the_Universe

No matter how detailed and prescriptive a company's processes are, smaller groups of employees will always need some level of self-organization to fulfill their tasks. Humans adapt, just like the bacteria in your gut. You should embrace this. By establishing a shared vision and a higher purpose, you can harness this self-organization and create something truly remarkable—together.

The time has come to leave the platform and travel into the core of the book. Hold on to your hat—here we go!

Staffan Nöteberg

staffan.noteberg@rekursiv.se

Part I

Setting the Foundation

In this first part, we embark on a journey to redefine how we think about strategic planning and goal-setting. We'll delve into the essential elements of a robust strategy, moving beyond the traditional confines of operational plans. We'll then explore the transformative potential of OKRs, not as mere performance metrics, but as guiding stars that illuminate a path toward meaningful change.

CHAPTER 1

Guiding Star Objectives

A guiding star is formulated as an *objective* and a few *key results*—a format inspired by the objectives and key results (OKR) framework. While the formulation itself is important, Part II of this book will reveal that crafting the objectives and the key results is merely one piece of the puzzle when it comes to achieving your long-term goals. The Guiding Star OKR framework also encompasses a comprehensive approach to work that creates a natural, continuous flow in which the aligned direction is always present and active throughout the organization.

In this chapter, we'll take a look at the *objective*, that is, the "O" in the OKR framework. You'll learn how objectives differ from everyday tasks and the key characteristics of objectives. You'll also learn how to use objectives as guiding principles for decision-making and how guiding star objectives are different from traditional OKR objectives. In the next chapter, we'll look at how the "KRs," or key results of OKRs, help us understand the objectives from multiple perspectives. But first, let's start with the end in mind.

Begin with the End in Mind

In the Guiding Star OKR framework, the first part of an OKR—the *objective*—is a captivating description of the future, such as "easy to buy." To reach our objective, we define two to five measurable properties called "key results." Together, our objective and its key results describe our current situation and the future state for which we strive, as shown in the image on page 4.

When crafting objectives, keep the following key characteristics in mind:

- An objective should be a concise and engaging narrative that resonates with everyone involved.

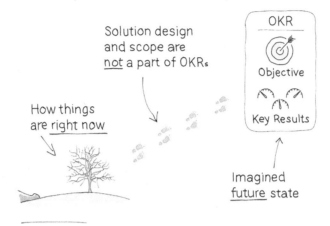

- An objective should be a vision of future outcomes that matter to customers, users, or other stakeholders beyond your team.

- An objective should focus on areas where you have significant control and influence rather than external factors like market share.

- An objective should show a clear contrast between the current reality and your aspirational future state.

- An objective should be a single, focused goal, not a collection of disparate objectives.

As you review these points, consider what a guiding star OKR is *not*:

- It's not a tech solution.
- It's not a list of activities.
- It's not a description of new features in our products.

This means that we begin with the end in mind. When unsure if you're following that principle, there's a good litmus test: if there's only one way to reach your objective, it's too narrow and short-term. Think bigger and further into the future.

Objectives as Engaging Campfire Stories

"Get outta here! That will be fantastic. How will you do that?"

You've just told a colleague about your objective, and this is the response you received. Your colleague is excited about the future you've conveyed and curious about how it will happen. The latter isn't obvious, but regardless of how, it would be "fantastic" if it succeeds. That's exactly the kind of reaction you want when you present your guiding star objective: excited and curious.

Imagine a story told around a campfire—it captures your attention, evokes emotions, and creates a sense of community among colleagues. Our goal to "reduce carbon emissions" becomes the story of "a greener future for generations to come."

A campfire story isn't a marketing slogan. The latter is designed to sell a product or service and is aimed at external audiences. While a slogan risks creating a superficial and short-term view of the company's ambitions, a campfire story is powerful for several reasons:

- *Engagement:* Stories capture our attention and make us more invested in the outcome.
- *Collaboration:* A shared story strengthens the sense of belonging and purpose.
- *Memorable:* Stories are easier to remember than simple facts and figures.
- *Creativity:* Stories open up new perspectives and ideas.

Objectives as Overarching Principles

Guiding star objectives fundamentally differ from traditional objectives. Take, for instance, a telecom company:

- *Traditional objective:* Launch 6G networks in 20 new cities.
- *Guiding star objective:* The world around me seamlessly blended with digital information and interactions, wherever I go.

The difference is clear: guiding star objectives are overarching principles that inform decision-making. Guiding star objectives are not tasks themselves, but rather the guiding lights that help us set the right course when defining specific work tasks. Think of them as our compass, ensuring that our execution stays true to our overarching strategy, rather than letting the day-to-day dictate our direction.

Additionally, guiding star objectives—expressed in the present tense—envision the shift in behavior that the user or customer will observe in the desired future state, rather than being an action list of what you must do right now. It's like the customer is speaking directly through a speech bubble. That's why, they're deliberately using the first-person pronoun—"I," "me," "my,"—which refers to the user or customer.

Imagine a truck manufacturer:

- *Traditional objective:* Redefine efficiency by delivering a reduction in fuel consumption across our flagship truck models.
- *Guiding star objective:* Less environmental impact for me as a truck owner.

In both examples, the guiding star objective transcends the immediate goal, focusing instead on the underlying value it provides.

Which option best aligns with our guiding star? That's the question that drives us forward.

Consider these two objectives for an insurance company. Which one would be more useful in guiding your decisions and priorities?

- *Traditional objective:* Proactively reduce claims through improved risk assessment and customer education programs.
- *Guiding star objective:* My accidents and injuries are prevented.

Objectives as a Direction, Not a Goal

Imagine a puzzle for which you have an exact picture or know what it should look like when finished, which pieces you have, and how you can move them. Small problems and recurring problems with near deadlines are often well structured like that. We know precisely what to do to achieve what we want.

Unfortunately, many problems we encounter in our complex businesses are ill-structured by nature: we don't know exactly what they will look like when they're finished, nor do we know the exact rules. Let's say you've just launched a new software product, and suddenly, users start reporting crashes. The problem is that there's no single error message, and it seems to happen in various scenarios. In this situation, you can't simply rely on your troubleshooting manual because every user's setup is different. It's worth noting that in complex environments, the rules might even unexpectedly shift—perhaps a recent operating system update is now conflicting with your software in ways you couldn't have anticipated. But with a guiding star objective, we believe we have a solid hypothesis about our desired direction, and we see no reason to delay progress while awaiting further information. Instead of focusing on arriving at a specific place, we choose to move in a meaningful direction. In this case, you choose to focus on improving overall software stability and compatibility rather than trying to fix every single crash report individually.

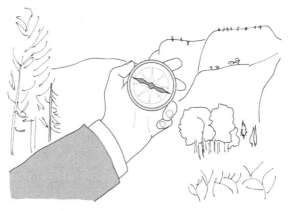

Take a moment to reflect on a current goal within your organization. Ask yourself:

- Why does this goal exist?
- What would be lost if we failed to achieve it?

The answers to these questions may reveal a deeper purpose, one that extends beyond immediate timelines or even your direct customers. They might touch on the needs of stakeholders further down the line—your customer's customer's customer—or speak to a broader value proposition. Consider replacing your current goal with the answers to these questions. The following are three examples.

A bank:

- *Traditional objective:* Become the preferred digital bank by growing our active digital user base.

- *Guiding star objective:* The freedom to manage my money whenever and wherever I want.

A tax authority:

- *Traditional objective:* Simplify tax filing for citizens by achieving an increase in digital tax return submissions.

- *Guiding star objective:* Easy for me as a citizen to file my taxes.

A company that develops industrial tools:

- *Traditional objective:* Dominate the market by capturing an additional market share within our target industry segment.

- *Guiding star objective:* Be a complete partner for me as a truck assembler.

Extending your goal horizon doesn't mean that you need to accomplish more within the same time frame. The true value lies not in reaching a specific destination as outlined in your plan but rather in the direction you choose, the pace at which you progress, and the overall quality of the outcome you cause.

The Fear of Outcome-Orientation

by: Joakim Manding Holm, Organizational Coach, Adaptiv

Sometimes, the most unlikely people resist using OKRs as intended. At a well-known, high-tech company, they wanted to introduce the OKR model—again! A few years back, I was told, they had rolled out OKRs across the organization but had rolled them back. The process around individual goals had led to excessive amounts of administrative work and dissatisfaction among the employees. This time around, individual OKRs were not required. Management emphasized the core ideas of dynamic goals, collaborative goal setting, and outcome-oriented key results.

When the time came to share our first batch of OKRs for my department, I was eager to hear the results. The product owner of each team stepped up and shared with the rest of the leads. To my confusion, what I heard were mostly deliveries and actions. "We will deliver feature X," said one PO. "We will do Y," said another. One guy said that they would "deliver documentation". When nudged by a department lead what they were trying to achieve, they responded "Well, better documentation!". All POs loudly objected to setting goals that were "not under their control."

I was surprised that it was the product owners that mostly resisted outcome-oriented goals. I (falsely) believed that they would welcome outcome-oriented goals with open arms since they would allow them and their teams the freedom to experiment.

These product owners were among the best and brightest so what caused this behavior? In retrospect, I suspect two forces. First of all, setting goals that you can only influence can feel strange and scary at first. People need time to get it right. Secondly, one must be very clear on if and how the OKRs would be used to assess performance (preferably only by experimental quality and effort – not actual results). When people suspect that their rating and compensation depend on them reaching their targets, they will prefer controllable key results.

Creating Guiding Star Objectives

To craft compelling and engaging stories for your guiding star objectives, follow these steps:

1. *Identify the protagonist.*

   If your objective were a story, who would be the main character? This could be your ideal customer, a specific user group, your organization, or even society. Consider whose behavior you aim to change or influence.

   Example: A young professional who is constantly on the move and needs to manage their finances seamlessly.

2. *Define their job-to-be-done (JTBD).[1]*

   What fundamental problem is your protagonist trying to solve? Focus on the "why" behind their actions, not only on the "how." What value do they seek to create, and for whom?

   Example: Have complete control over his or her money, being able to access accounts, make payments, and track spending anytime, anywhere, and without any hassle.

3. *Imagine alternative solutions.*

   How could the protagonist achieve their JTBD in a different way? Challenge assumptions and explore unconventional paths. Embrace "what if" scenarios to spark creative and innovative ideas.

   Example: Beyond traditional online banking, they could benefit from a mobile app with advanced features like real-time spending notifications, budgeting tools, and even personalized financial insights.

4. *Envision a successful outcome.*

   Paint a vivid picture of how the world will look once the protagonist adopts a new approach. What positive impact will this change have on them and others?

   Example: With a user-friendly and comprehensive mobile banking app, the young professional feels empowered and in control of private finances, making informed decisions and achieving financial goals with ease.

---

1. https://www.youtube.com/watch?v=StcObeAxavY

5. *Weave your objective into a narrative.*

    Using the elements you've gathered, craft a concise story that encapsulates your objective. Let the protagonist speak. Connect it to your core values to make it even more impactful.

    Example: The freedom to manage my money whenever and wherever I want.

To create an effective objective story, keep the following in mind:

- *Keep it concise.* Focus on the core message and avoid overwhelming the narrative with details. Remember, you're not explaining "how" at this stage.

- *Choose neutral language.* Avoid words whose sole purpose is to amplify, like "world-class." Your focus is on providing transparency to those interested in this direction. You aim to inform, not persuade.

- *Welcome feedback.* Share your story with colleagues and actively seek their input. Diverse perspectives can significantly enhance your narrative. For a more comprehensive understanding, consider developing multiple versions to compare feedback.

Fostering a culture of learning and support within your organization is another success factor. Provide resources and training on storytelling techniques, document best practices, and ensure that experts are readily available to offer guidance and coaching.

Urgent ≠ Important

Imagine a forest as a company. In the forest, there are many different animals and plants, all with their own jobs to do. Some jobs are urgent, such as when a squirrel gathers nuts for the winter. It's important that the squirrel gets this job done before the snow comes; otherwise, it might not survive.

Other jobs are important but not as urgent. A tree grows slowly and absorbs carbon dioxide from the air. This is important for the whole forest and the planet, but it doesn't happen overnight.

It's the same in a company. Some tasks are urgent, such as meeting a customer contract deadline or upgrading software before vendor support expires. Other tasks are important for the company's long-term success, like developing new products or improving the company's environmental impact.

Don't confuse *urgent* with *unplanned*. A bug report might be a critical production incident requiring immediate action, or it could simply be a single user's request for a nonessential feature.

It's crucial to understand the difference between urgent and important, both in the forest and at work. If we only focus on what's urgent—we are deadline-driven—we might miss what's important in the long run and instead get stuck in an endless cycle of firefighting. A fashion retail company could formulate a long-term objective like this:

- *Traditional objective:* Launch a sustainable collection.
- *Guiding star objective:* Fashion and sustainability go hand in hand.

Striking a balance between urgent and important tasks is key to long-term success. Guiding stars specifically address what's important but not yet urgent—transformative work and investments in entirely new capabilities that you need to start today to avoid putting out fires in twelve or eighteen months. Rest assured that your day-to-day operations, maintenance, and other essential tasks won't be neglected, even if they're not directly highlighted by your guiding stars. You'll see in Chapter 5, Pupation: Integrating Guiding Stars with Agile Planning, on page 55, how to incorporate these long-term objectives into your agile workflow, ensuring they align seamlessly with your everyday tasks.

Guiding Stars at Different Levels

You will discover how guiding stars can be initiated from different levels within an organization in Chapter 4, Catchball: Defining Guiding Stars Cross-Collaboratively, on page 41. Guiding stars on multiple levels is *not* like a project breakdown where the project director is delegating isolated nonviable tasks to each team simply to make the tasks fit like cogs in a larger machine. From the team's perspective, they're a small company making their customers' and users' work easier and more efficient.

Consider a development team setting a guiding star. Typically, a team operates at a faster pace than, say, an entire department. In this context, a guiding star OKR would be equivalent to a sprint goal in Scrum, representing the team's most crucial objective for the next one to two weeks.

Here are some examples of what a goal set by an individual team might look like:

- *Telecom:* My connection is reliable in the woods.
- *Automotive:* I can easily track my fuel consumption.
- *Insurance:* I feel safer and more protected.
- *Banking:* I can easily stay on top of my spending.
- *Government:* Filing my taxes is simple and stress-free.
- *Industrial tools:* I can quickly get the help I need.
- *Retail:* My eco-friendly options are highlighted, making it easier to make sustainable choices.

The objectives in these examples intentionally use first-person pronouns like "I," "me," and "my" to emphasize the user's or customer's perspective. This isn't the place to detail features or requirements. The purpose is to align the team's direction. Features and requirements probably reside in the team's backlog, derived from the guiding stars.

Managing Potential Priority Conflicts

It's common for questions about priorities to arise when time, money, and other resources are insufficient for all goals within the organization.

By definition, your guiding stars cannot be prioritized against each other. If the need for prioritization arises, it means you have too many guiding stars. Typically, a guiding star sponsor (role described in Chapter 4, Catchball: Defining Guiding Stars Cross-Collaboratively, on page 41) manages between one and three guiding stars at a time—never more. Think of it as selecting strategies and prioritizing execution.

Key Takeaways

- Guiding Star OKR is a framework for formulating long-term goals, encompassing a complete way of working to create a natural and continuous flow in which goals are present throughout the organization.

- A guiding star objective is a captivating description of the future, different from traditional objectives, and serves as a guiding principle for decision-making.

- Guiding star objectives should be formulated as engaging stories that everyone can understand and appreciate, focusing on future results valued by customers or users.

- Formulating objectives as campfire stories enhances engagement, meaning-making, memorability, and communication.

- Guiding star objectives are not solutions, activity lists, or feature descriptions but rather a direction toward a future state.

- Guiding star objectives represent the "important but not yet urgent" aspects of work, focusing on transformative work and investments in new capabilities.

- Guiding stars cannot be prioritized against each other; if the need for prioritization arises, it indicates having too many guiding stars.

What's Next?

Now that you understand objectives and how they differ from daily tasks, it's time to set key results to help you achieve these objectives. The next chapter will teach you how key results quantify and refine your objectives. You'll see that key results aren't about proving you've reached the objective, but about understanding what the objective truly means.

CHAPTER 2

Guiding Star Key Results

Using quantitative examples—target numbers—when communicating your future vision can be a powerful tool. Not only do these key results (the "KR" in an OKR) ensure that the organization agrees on the objective (the "O" in an OKR) it's striving for, but they also provide a more aligned understanding of the objective in practical terms. Additionally, these numbers make it easier for stakeholders to grasp the vision's consequences and potential impacts.

In this chapter, you'll learn what key results are, what they should and should not include, and how they relate to the objective. You'll also learn some best practices for writing key results and how (and why) guiding star key results differ from traditional OKR key results. Let's start with the most fundamental question.

What Is a Key Result?

In the previous chapter, we established that objectives are qualitative outcomes that envision a shift in behavior. Key results, on the other hand, are the observable or measurable properties—the quantitative results—that indicate that this outcome has occurred. It's important to emphasize that these key results are *the result of*—not the cause of—the change we want to see. That's why the acronym OKR ends with "R."

For example, consider the objective, "A dinner enjoyed by everyone." A possible key result might be, "The carrot plate on the kitchen table is empty." One cause of this outcome is, of course, that we cooked a delicious meal, as shown in the image on page 16.

A Variable

You may think of the key result as a variable. The moment you decide to work toward a guiding star, the variable has a starting value (X), and if you achieve

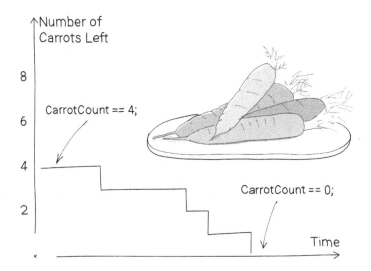

your objective, the key result will have a target value (Y) at that time. So you can format the key results as follows:

```
[property metric]: from [starting value] to [target value]
```

Although achieving your target value is important, monitoring the journey is equally valuable. Key results help you observe change as you develop viable features designed to realize your objective. This monitoring provides input for prioritizing ongoing tasks and making decisions about whether to adjust key results along the way.

Not Activities

Note that key results are not tasks. The insurance company that formulated its objective in the previous chapter as "My accidents and injuries are prevented" could have the following key results:

- Percentage of customers using preventive safety features in the app: from X% to Y%.

- Number of accidents among insured drivers: from X to Y.

- Average claim cost per accident: from X dollars to Y dollars.

Intentionally, none of these three examples clearly state what that insurance company should do, since tasks are defined later in the company's agile planning. Tasks cause change; they're not the result of it. Therefore, never start a key result with verbs like launch, create, develop, deliver, build, make, implement, define, test, prepare, or plan. Don't even start with increase or reduce, as the desired direction of change is implied by comparing the target value Y to the baseline X.

The combination of a single objective and two to five corresponding key results forms a guiding star OKR—that is, a desired outcome and two to five properties that should emerge as a result of that outcome.

Remember, although key results quantify and concretize your guiding star, the objective ultimately determines success. Key results are indicators—not definitive proof—that your objective has been met.

The Short Answer

The short answer to the question, "What's a key result?" is:

- a property metric of your objective that
- has a starting value (X) today and
- later has a different target value (Y) that is
- a result of the objective being achieved.

Let's put this theory into practice with some examples.

Telecom Company:

- *Objective:* The world around me seamlessly blended with digital information and interactions, wherever I go.

- *Key result 1:* Percentage of users accessing and utilizing personalized AI-powered services: from X% to Y%.

- *Key result 2:* Number of new innovative applications and services developed by third-party developers leveraging the 6G network: from X to Y.

Tax Authority:

- *Objective:* Easy for me as a citizen to file my taxes.

- *Key result 1:* Average time to complete a digital tax return: from X minutes to Y minutes.

- *Key result 2:* Number of incorrect tax returns: from X to Y.

Industrial Tools Company:

- *Objective:* Be a complete partner for me as a truck assembler.

- *Key result 1:* Delivery time for customized tools: from X days to Y days.

- *Key result 2:* Percentage of customers using the company's digital support platform: from X% to Y%.

Purpose-Driven Development

Imagine a company, Michaní, Inc., that consistently falls behind its competitor, Astéria, Inc. The sequence in which each company addresses its purpose, metrics, and activities differs:

- *Astéria, Inc.:* Determine purpose (direction) → Define metrics → Plan tasks
- *Michaní, Inc.:* Plan tasks → Define metrics → Determine purpose (direction)

This difference has significant consequences when the two companies develop their personal finance apps.

Astéria begins by defining the purpose ("users gain control of their finances"). Then, it defines metrics to quantitatively monitor that journey ("increased savings rate," "reduced debt levels"). Finally, it plans tasks that directly contribute to these metrics ("develop a budgeting tool," "integrate with bank accounts for automatic tracking"). The result is an app focused on creating value for users by empowering them to make informed financial decisions.

Michaní operates in a reverse sequence. It starts by planning tasks ("create a flashy UI," "implement cryptocurrency trading"). It then defines metrics ("number of app downloads," "average time spent in the app"). Finally, it tries to find a purpose that fits these tasks and metrics. The result might be an app with many features but without a clear focus on users' financial well-being or goals.

Organizations that operate like Michaní usually engage in tasks that are based on old habits, a will to copy competitors, or a vague notion of a potential future benefit.

You probably noticed that Michaní's last two steps—defining its metrics and purpose—are a waste of time, as its tasks are already planned in the first step. Unfortunately, the vision is reverse-engineered.

In guiding star OKRs, you always start by setting the purpose. This purpose informs the choice of metrics, and only after the metrics are defined do you consider the question of "How?", that is, which tasks to plan, as shown in the image on page 19.

The purpose—the direction—is your objective (the "O" in an OKR), and the metrics are your key results (the "KR" in an OKR). Based on that, tasks are defined in the agile planning.

Never engage in setting objectives or key results when tasks are already determined.

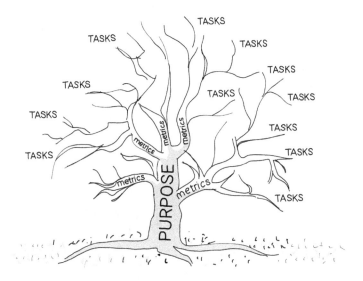

How Key Results Relate to Agile Planning, Calibration, Catchball, Cross-Pollination, Discovery, and Objectives

In our messy reality, relationships between things are often as important as the things themselves. To understand the relationship between key results and various processes, see these chapters:

- New knowledge from Discovery often influences your objectives and your key results (see Chapter 3, Discovering Customer Opportunities, on page 29).

- You develop your objectives and your key results collaboratively in the Catchball process (see Chapter 4, Catchball: Defining Guiding Stars Cross-Collaboratively, on page 41).

- Where the rubber meets the road, new insights may arise that lead you to adjust your key results in Calibration (see Chapter 6, Calibration: Fine-Tuning Guiding Stars, on page 65).

- By keeping your key results alive and top of everyone's mind with Cross-Pollination, you reduce the risk of "set-and-forget" (see Chapter 7, Cross-Pollination: Everyone's Ears, Insights, and Ideas, on page 79).

- The order of operations is crucial when you define and plan objectives (see Chapter 1, Guiding Star Objectives, on page 3), key results (this chapter), and viable features (see Chapter 5, Pupation: Integrating Guiding Stars with Agile Planning, on page 55).

Even the world's best key results have no value if they don't integrate well with the other processes in the Guiding Star OKR framework.

Key Results Indicate, They Don't Prove

Imagine you've planted a beautiful flower bed in your garden. To protect it from hungry deer, you've put up a fence around the bed. A month later, you go out to inspect the results. You see that the flowers are thriving and the leaves are green and healthy.

Your observation indicates that the fence may have had a positive effect. The flowers don't appear to have been eaten, suggesting that the deer haven't been able to get into the bed.

But the observation doesn't definitively prove that it was the fence that protected the flowers. There could be other explanations. Perhaps the deer weren't interested in yellow flowers, or maybe it happened to be a period when they stayed away from the garden for other reasons.

Similarly, in product development, knowing exactly what causes success is difficult due to the complex nature of collaboration and knowledge-intensive work. Quantitative metrics can be helpful indicators, but they don't always tell the whole story.

A company might see an improvement in the quality of its apps six months after investing in an automated testing tool. Its key results show fewer bugs, higher user ratings, and more downloads.

But as with the flower bed and the fence, we can't be entirely sure that the automated testing tool is the sole cause. Perhaps its development team has become better at coding, or maybe user expectations have changed.

Another company that develops an app for truck maintenance defines this OKR as follows:

- *Objective:* It's easy for me as a mechanic to navigate the app.
- *Key result:* Maximum number of clicks to reach any feature: from 10 down to 4.

After hard work, the development teams achieve the key result. But when the company asks customers and its own product managers if they think the app has become easier to navigate, the answer is no.

The focus on reducing clicks might have missed the mark. User-friendliness might be more about finding the right feature quickly, even if it takes a few extra clicks. Issues such as illogical menus or unfamiliar terminology could also be contributing factors.

The examples with the flowers and the testing tool show that key results can be useful for indicating progress along the way. In a large organization, they can also serve as a unifying picture of what an objective truly means, even before the change work has begun. Having multiple key results—ideally two to five—further enriches that unified picture. But key results don't guarantee success.

Combining quantitative measurements with qualitative feedback from users and stakeholders provides a more comprehensive understanding. Remember, the objective is paramount, regardless of whether key results are achieved.

The "Easy to Measure" Fallacy

You might have heard of Nasreddin Hodja, a beloved figure from the 13th-century Muslim world. He once lost his key in the dark but stubbornly searched for it under a streetlight. When asked why, he replied, "It's brighter here." This parable is an analogy with a common pitfall: focusing on what's easiest to measure rather than what's most relevant.

It's easy to think of key results as simple, standalone metrics, like the number of defects in a product. But key results are more powerful when they capture your objective's relationship to products, people, trends, companies, or whatever.

The tax authority with the goal of making tax filing easier for citizens could track a metric like the average time it takes to file a return. But what if they wanted to understand the experience for a specific group, like parents of young children who also have a mortgage?

- *Context-Free Key Result:* Tax-filing time for citizens.
- *Relational Key Result:* Tax-filing time for parents of young children with a mortgage: from X to Y.

By creating a key result that focuses on this specific group, you gain a much clearer picture of how well you're meeting their needs. Consider what surrounds your objective when you author your key results: children, houses, or other relevant things. Relational key results connect the dots between your goals and the things that matter most. While they might require more effort to track, the insights they provide are invaluable. Don't be Nasreddin Hodja.

For example, if you're launching a new product with modular features, you might track the percentage of customers who purchase related products or services after their initial purchase. This key result reveals not only the product's success but also its ability to integrate with your customers' broader needs and workflows.

Ultimately, the best key results are those that tell a story. They go beyond simple numbers and reveal the nuances of your progress.

Key Results Cannot Be Delegated

A WBS[1] (work breakdown structure) is a valuable tool for managing projects, much like a recipe is essential for baking a cake. A recipe outlines clear steps, ingredient order, and mixing techniques, with each step contributing to the final delicious result.

But applying this project-oriented mindset to strategic directions can lead to a common misconception: viewing key results as independent tasks that, once completed, automatically fulfill the overall objective. Forcing traditional project management methods into OKR is sometimes referred to as "cascading OKRs." The term "cascade" derives from the Italian word "cascata," meaning "waterfall," perhaps implying a top-down flow of objectives. I strongly advise against this practice when you work with long-term goals like OKRs.

Strategic directions are not projects. They're more like journeys guided by a star, with potential obstacles, detours, and evolving paths. Each decision and action is interconnected, shaping the ongoing voyage. Approaching your strategic work with overly front-loaded projects makes persistence stifle adaptability. This undermines the trifecta balance (see Balancing the Trifecta of Strategic Execution, on page xiv).

---

1.   https://www.pmi.org/learning/library/work-breakdown-structure-basic-principles-4883

Let's consider a key result example from the fashion retail industry. Imagine a company with the following OKR:

- *Objective:* Fashion and sustainability go hand in hand.

- *Key result 1:* Percentage of sustainable materials in new collections: from X% to Y%.

- *Key result 2:* Number of recognitions from external sustainability organizations: from X to Y.

Assigning key result 1 solely to the design team and key result 2 to the sales team could create unforeseen challenges. The design team might not prioritize collaborating with sustainability organizations when working with material choices, unaware of the potential impact on partnerships. Conversely, the sales team might focus on securing recognitions without fully understanding the complexities of sustainable material sourcing.

The key results are interconnected. The design team's material choices directly influence which sustainability organizations will recognize the company's efforts. So, why not let the design team and the sales team share the same objective and key results? Achieving both key results requires collaboration, shared understanding, and a holistic approach.

Key results are results (hence the name)—not isolated tasks—of the overarching objective. Delegating key results individually can lead to fragmented efforts and hinder overall success.

When Will We Celebrate?

You might have experienced a manager who wants to create a positive and motivating culture in which achievements are recognized and rewarded. Following the "carrot and stick" approach, major project deliveries are celebrated. But for individual teams or employees, project deliveries might not hold the same significance as they do for the manager.

Sometimes, managers may even personally have monetary bonuses tied to achieving key results. This should be avoided at all costs as it can create conflicts of interest, making managers hesitant to adjust goals based on new information, even if it benefits the company. They don't want to lose their bonus.

The Guiding Star OKR framework is built on the idea that intrinsic motivation comes from attributes such as autonomy, mastery, purpose, growth, and social interaction. The good news is that intrinsic motivation naturally creates small celebrations all the time and precisely for those who find it relevant.

Catchball, Calibration, and Cross-Pollination are examples of contexts that foster autonomy, mastery, purpose, growth, and social interaction, and are all topics covered later in this book.

Facilitating an OKR Draft Brainstorming Session

With the Guiding Star OKR framework, the goal is to capture the entire organization's observations and interpretations of reality. So you don't develop your objectives and your key results in a single session, from start to finish. But it can be helpful to quickly brainstorm an initial draft. Here's one way to do that:

1. *Gather a cross-functional group.*
   Since this session won't involve any final decisions, there's no need to be concerned about decision-making authority or political alliances. Everyone who wants to participate should be invited, and don't delay the session simply because a key person can't make it.

2. *Generate all objectives using the 1-2-All workshop method [LM14].*
   This facilitation technique involves participants initially reflecting individually and writing down their ideas. Then, the ideas are discussed and developed in pairs before the entire group selects and refines them together.

3. *Take one objective at a time, and brainstorm two to five properties that express the results of that specific objective being realized.*
   In this step, you may also work according to the 1-2-All method. Ignore the starting and target values of your key results for now. Focus only on formulating the metric and evaluating it with the seven concept-checking questions listed in *Concept-Checking Questions for Key Results*.

4. *Divide the responsibility for proposing starting and target values.*
   This work continues after the meeting and involves talking to experts about where you're now and where you want to go.

The "All" part of 1-2-All usually yields even better results if it has a structured method, such as *Six Thinking Hats [de 85]* or Ritual Dissent.[2]

---

2. https://cynefin.io/wiki/Ritual_dissent

In step 2, you identify all your objectives before even considering the key results in step 3. This is because your objectives need to be interconnected and reflect what's most important—not urgent—at this time.

In Chapter 4, Catchball: Defining Guiding Stars Cross-Collaboratively, on page 41, you'll explore *catchball*, a process used to align and communicate goals across different organizational levels and departments.

Concept-Checking Questions for Key Results

To validate your key results, ask yourself the following questions:

1. *Quantitative*: Does the key result answer the question "how much" or "how many" using specific numbers rather than the Boolean values true and false?

2. *Concise and specific*: Is the key result free of jargon, abbreviations, and technical terms, ensuring that everyone can understand it without additional explanation?

3. *Outcome-oriented*: Does the key result focus on the desired result or outcome, rather than the tasks required to achieve it or the resources invested?

4. *Limited in number*: Are there two to five key results per objective, ensuring focus?

5. *Customer-centric*: Does the key result reflect a change in customer behavior or experience, indicating that we are meeting their needs?

6. *Non-incentivized*: Is the key result independent of any incentives or performance evaluations, ensuring that it focuses on the desired outcome rather than personal gain?

7. *Broadly relevant*: Is the key result relevant to a wide range of stakeholders, potentially involving the entire cross-functional product team or product area?

Key Takeaways

- Unlike the qualitative nature of objectives, key results are measurable values that show whether the desired outcome has been achieved. They're the effect—not the cause—of the change you want to see.

- Think of key results as variables that change over time. They have an initial value (X) and a target value (Y), which is reached when the objective is met. Monitoring these values helps track progress.

- Key results are helpful indicators, but they don't definitively prove that an objective is met. Complex situations often have multiple influencing factors.

- Focus on key results that truly reflect the desired outcome, even if they're harder to measure. Don't fall into the trap of prioritizing easy but less meaningful metrics.

- Avoid assigning individual key results to separate teams as if they were project tasks. Strategic directions are journeys, not projects, and key results require a holistic approach.

- Instead of focusing on extrinsic rewards tied to project deliveries, foster an environment that promotes intrinsic motivation through autonomy, mastery, purpose, growth, and social interaction.

- Gather a diverse group and use techniques like the 1-2-All method to generate initial objectives and key result ideas. Refine them later through expert input and further discussion.

What's Next?

Having covered objectives (previous chapter) and key results (this chapter), the next chapter will show you how to set guiding star OKRs that focus on entirely new customer capabilities, rather than simply adding features and improving existing products. It emphasizes that understanding your customers' customers' jobs-to-be-done is key to setting effective guiding stars.

Part II

Guiding Stars in Action

Having established the foundation, we now turn our attention to the practical application of the Guiding Star OKR framework. This part will equip you with the tools and techniques to uncover transformative customer opportunities, foster collaborative goal-setting, and seamlessly integrate strategic aspirations with your existing agile planning. We'll also explore how to adapt and evolve your guiding stars through calibration and cross-pollination, ensuring your organization remains agile and responsive in the face of change.

CHAPTER 3

Discovering Customer Opportunities

Product discovery is a broad field that includes various methods for gathering insights, ranging from interviews and observations to data analysis and experiments. Some of these methods help companies understand their customers' ecosystem from the inside, which is key to creating products and services that not only meet articulated requirements but also provide innovative solutions and new capabilities that truly benefit customers.

Kathy Sierra captured the essence of that approach—to give the customer new capabilities, not new features—in her book, *Badass: Making Users Awesome [Sie15]*: "Don't just upgrade your product, upgrade your users. Don't make a better power drill, make a better home DIY builder."

In this chapter, we'll explore how to create an effective *Opportunities and Outcomes (O&O)* artifact, a resource in which you collect specific information from your product discovery work. While the purpose of your guiding star OKRs is to create alignment, persistence, and adaptability by charting a course forward for your organization, it's the O&O that forms the basis for choosing these guiding stars in the catchball process.

What Is the Opportunities and Outcomes Artifact?

The O&O artifact is a central resource in the Guiding Star OKR framework. It explains why your customers pull your products and services into their lives. It also answers questions about your customers' value chain, market landscape, and technological trends that affect them. This information helps you avoid getting stuck in old patterns and encourages innovative thinking.

The main use of an O&O artifact is to provide essential input when you select your guiding stars in the catchball process (see Chapter 4, Catchball: Defining Guiding Stars Cross-Collaboratively, on page 41). The O&O is also a valuable tool for internal communication, ensuring that everyone in your organization shares a common understanding of the customer's context. By making the O&O artifact available to everyone in the organization, you create a culture of openness and participation. This increases understanding of your guiding stars and the motivation to work together towards them.

In an organization with a weak customer focus—one that's primarily driven by projects and budgets—it's even more beneficial to invest time and energy in formulating and communicating the O&O artifact. Everyone in the organization, regardless of their role or department, contributes directly or indirectly to creating value for the customer and ultimately to the organization's success. Understanding the problem you're trying to solve for the customer empowers the employees to make the right micro-decisions on a daily basis.

It's important to understand that the O&O isn't something that you create once and then archive, like a project pre-study. Neither is the O&O updated hastily before each catchball. It's a living and dynamic artifact that you continuously evolve as your customer and its environment change. From the first hesitant steps of a product idea to the launch, growth, and eventual retirement of the product, the O&O artifact continues to be a central source of knowledge and insights.

The Guiding Star OKR framework is designed to be iterative, with each cycle kicking off with catchball. Discovery, in general, and the O&O artifact, in particular, aren't confined to a specific iteration. Your understanding of customers and their markets is naturally going to evolve over time. Wherever you're in a given cycle, make sure you're working with the most up-to-date version of your O&O.

If you agree the purpose of the O&O is to establish a strong foundation for selecting effective guiding stars, you're likely wondering what specific content this artifact contains. An O&O offers a comprehensive view of your customer and your customer's environment. It's usually divided into five sections:

1. *The Customer's Job Statements*
   The O&O begins with job statements developed collaboratively with the customer. These describe what the customer truly wants to achieve and in what situations—not how they use your products.

2. *The Customer's Value Chain*
   Next, a Wardley map[1] helps you understand your customer's value chain and how your products interact with others to create your

---

1.   https://www.youtube.com/watch?v=KkePAhnkHeg

customer's products and services. It provides an overview of which components are important to the customer and their maturity stage.

3. *Tech Trends and the Customer's Market*

    The third section is an analysis of your customer's market and potential growth opportunities. Look at trends, competition, and other factors that could impact their success. You should also investigate relevant technological trends that could affect their operations and create new opportunities for innovation.

4. *The Customer's Opportunities*

    This section highlights instances where the customer experiences obstacles, frustrations, or workarounds. Eliminating a pain point represents an opportunity. Formulate opportunities from the customer's negative quotes, such as, "I have to restart the entire system to update the generated forecasts." Your goal isn't simply to eliminate waste but to empower the customer with new capabilities that make these problems irrelevant.

5. *The Customer's Outcomes*

    The final section describes the customer's desired future. What could their situation look like if the challenges you identified no longer existed? What new possibilities would open up? Focus on the customer's experience, not on your products.

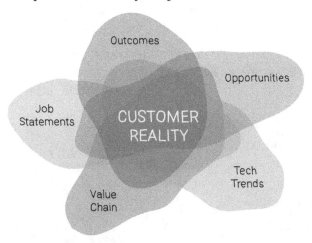

In the remainder of this chapter, we'll take a closer look at each of the five O&O sections. As you read, I encourage you to reflect on how this information can help you better define your long-term goals, that is, your guiding stars.

Let's start with what's known as *job statements*.

Discovering the Customer's Job Statements

The first section of the O&O outlines the customer's job statements, a concept borrowed from the Jobs-to-Be-Done (JTBD) framework.[2] While it's widely accepted that products have features, that features solve specific problems for customers, and that customers belong to various segments (demographic, psychographic, geographic, and so on), might there be better ways to categorize the effect the product has on people's lives?

In *Competing Against Luck [Chr16]*, author Clayton Christensen introduces JTBD as a new way to understand customer behavior and innovation. While traditional approaches examine the parts—features, solutions, and customer segments—JTBD focuses on value-creating interactions between these and other elements. A key analysis, for example, is the situation in which the customer wants to achieve a specific outcome.

Imagine it's dinnertime and you're rushing to get food ready for your hungry family. You're in the kitchen with a pile of potatoes that need peeling. You "hire" a potato peeler to achieve the following "progress": from having unpeeled potatoes to peeled potatoes ready for cooking while minimizing the risk of injury and food waste.

When we use a product, we are essentially "hiring" it to do a job for us. If the product does the job well, we will gladly hire it again when the same need arises. But if it falls short of expectations, we "fire" it and look for something else that can solve the problem better.

The company that makes the potato peeler could improve its sharpness, grip, and safety. But perhaps they should also ask themselves if you—the customer—must "hire" a potato peeler to achieve this "progress."

Examples of Job Statements

A statement for the potato job may be formulated as, "When I'm cooking dinner for my family, I want to minimize food waste so that buying ingredients doesn't become unnecessarily expensive for the family." Let's generalize this sentence into a template for job statements:

```
When I [situation],

I want [motivation]

so that I [outcome].
```

---

2.   https://www.youtube.com/watch?v=StcObeAxavY

You answer three questions:

1. What's the customer's context?
2. What does the customer want in that context?
3. Why does the customer want it?

Are job statements limited to consumer products like potato peelers? Absolutely not. Let's explore how they can be applied in a business-to-business context by examining a company that develops integrated hardware and software solutions.

Trusted Tools is a company that develops and manufactures industrial tools. One of their customers is the truck manufacturer Beza Trucks. The tool Beza uses is a high-precision nutrunner that also stores information—such as how many turns each bolt has been tightened during engine assembly—in the cloud for traceability.

After talking to their customer Beza Trucks, Trusted Tools develops three job statement proposals:

1. When I assemble engines (situation), I want to ensure that each bolt is tightened with the correct torque and that all data on the bolt tightening are logged (motivation), so that I can guarantee the highest quality and avoid costly production errors (outcome).

2. When I present our production process to customers and partners (situation), I want to be able to show that we use the latest technology and take quality seriously (motivation), so that we strengthen our brand and reputation as a reliable truck manufacturer (outcome).

3. When I optimize our engine production (situation), I want a tool that helps us streamline the process while maintaining the highest quality (motivation), so that we can reduce costs and increase profitability without compromising safety or performance (outcome).

It's the customer's (Beza Trucks') voice that we hear, even though it's the supplier (Trusted Tools) who formulates these job statements.

Concepts of Job Statements

By now, you might be wondering how Trusted Tools conjures up these well-crafted statements. To understand this, let's explore the core concepts that shape their approach.

The Job, Not the Product
> Beza Trucks isn't interested in the nutrunner itself but in the ability to assemble engines efficiently, reliably, and traceably. Their "job" is to ensure high-quality engines and avoid costly production errors or recalls.

Dimensions
> *Functional:* The nutrunner must be powerful and precise enough to tighten bolts with the correct torque. Data collection must be reliable and easily accessible.
>
> *Emotional:* Beza Trucks wants to feel confident and secure that their engines are correctly assembled. The tool should contribute to a sense of control and professionalism.
>
> *Social:* By using an advanced tool with traceability, Beza Trucks can demonstrate to their customers and partners that they take quality seriously. This can strengthen their brand and reputation.

Progress
> Beza Trucks "hires" Trusted Tools' nutrunner to make progress in their production process. They want to move from having loose engine parts to having finished, tested, and documented engines. The nutrunner is a tool that helps them achieve that goal.

Competition
> Trusted Tools' nutrunner competes not only with other nutrunners but also with other ways to assemble engines. Beza Trucks could use manual tools, automated robots, or entirely different assembly methods. To remain competitive, the nutrunner must offer Beza, in this specific situation, a unique value that other options can't match, such as the combination of precision, traceability, and user-friendliness.

Creating Job Statements

We've explored some examples of job statements Trusted Tools created in their O&O artifact about Beza Trucks. We've also taken a closer look at the general concepts behind the JTBD theory. To conclude, let's review the five-step process the Trusted Tools team uses to develop new job statements:

1. *Interview and observe.*

   Trusted Tools conducts in-depth interviews with Beza Trucks staff, asking open-ended questions like, "What are the biggest challenges you face during engine assembly?" or "What would make your job easier?" They might also observe workers on the assembly line, noting their interactions with the nutrunner and any frustrations or workarounds.

2. *Identify jobs.*

   Based on these interviews and observations, Trusted Tools identifies the underlying needs Beza Trucks is trying to satisfy. They might discover, for example, that the primary job isn't only about tightening bolts, but about ensuring the highest quality engine assembly possible.

3. *Categorize jobs.*

   These jobs are then categorized into functional ("Tightening bolts accurately"), emotional ("Feeling confident in the assembly process"), and social ("Projecting a positive image of quality to customers") dimensions. This ensures a holistic understanding of Beza Truck's world.

4. *Develop job statements.*

   Trusted Tools creates clear and concise job statements for each identified need. These statements follow the format: "When I [situation], I want to [motivation], so I can [outcome]." For example, "When I assemble engines, I want to ensure that each bolt is tightened with the correct torque, so I can guarantee the highest quality and avoid costly production errors."

5. *Validate job statements.*

   Trusted Tools shares these job statements with Beza Trucks, seeking feedback and confirmation that they accurately reflect Beza's reality. This step ensures that the final job statements are truly customer-centric.

If your team has absolutely no way to communicate directly with your customer, you may collaborate with sales representatives, account managers, product managers, or other internal stakeholders who can act as proxies for the customer. While far from ideal, it's better than nothing.

Pensioners Prefer Traditional Letters Over Digital Forms

by: Martin Christensen, author of Holistic Product Discovery

"The form used when applying for housing supplements for pensioners, etc., is perceived by many as complicated and difficult to handle. When processing the form, many applications need to be corrected, which some explain is due to the form's construction. A potential solution is to create an interactive and intelligent form on the web." – Swedish Pensions Agency

There was a disconnect between pensioners and the application form, a fact established by the agency's numerous calls with their customers. When interviewing and observing pensioners, my team discovered that the reasons for the gap were more complex than anticipated. Many customers perceived the act of sending the form as impersonal, as it involved officially asking for help in an emotional situation. Additionally, they felt unsure about the accuracy of their completed form, leading to a sense of insecurity.

A limitation of the project was that the form would not be completely digitized from the start—a digital signature solution was planned for a potential second phase, contingent on the success of the initial version. Hence, the first solution idea was to create a step-by-step question-naire on the web and then just output the result into the preexisting form. Therefore, we quickly understood that we had to take the underlying reasons for impersonality and insecurity into consideration as well.

At that time, the pensioners were comfortable with writing personal letters and vouching for the content of these with their signatures, so we opted for outputting the result in the form of a traditional letter.

The outcome of the project was that the pensioners felt more confident and supported, the number of applications that needed to be corrected was significantly reduced, and it was decided to fully digitize this form and several others like it.

Mapping Your Customer's Value Chain

The second section of the O&O is a Wardley map—a visual strategic model used to analyze and understand how your customer creates value for their customers. It shows how different components of their offerings evolve over time and how they relate to each other.

Remember the potato peeler from earlier in this chapter? This time, imagine that the company manufacturing that tool is your customer, and you're creating Wardley maps with the following content:

- *Value chain:* The steps their users take to peel potatoes, from choosing a peeler to having peeled potatoes ready for use.

- *Components:* The different parts of the potato peeler, such as the blade, handle, and any additional features.

- *Evolution:* How these components evolve over time, from being new and innovative to becoming more standardized and widely available.

- *Visibility:* How visible the different components are to their customers, from the most obvious (like the blade) to the more hidden (like material choices or manufacturing processes).

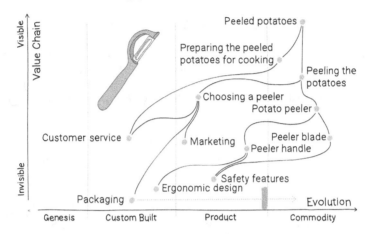

Studying these Wardley maps can yield several insights:

- *Focus on the job, not the product:* You realize your customer's customers don't want a potato peeler; they want peeled potatoes quickly, safely, and efficiently.

- *Opportunities for innovation:* You see the potential to develop new solutions that don't necessarily involve a traditional potato peeler.

- *Competitive advantages:* You can identify areas where they can differentiate themselves by offering unique solutions that better meet their customers' needs.

- *Outsourcing noncore:* It may be more efficient to purchase certain components in your value chain as commodities rather than investing resources in developing them in-house.

In a biological ecosystem, two or more species often influence each other's evolution over time. One example is the relationship between flowering plants and pollinating insects. Flowers have evolved colorful petals and nectar to attract insects, while insects have developed specialized body parts to collect pollen and nectar. This mutual adaptation benefits both parties: insects get food, and plants get help with pollination, leading to reproduction and the spread of their genes.

Coevolution is also crucial in business value chains. The insights gained from your customer's Wardley maps can spark ideas for how you need to develop your own products to remain a valuable partner to your customer.

Unfortunately, the details of creating a Wardley map are beyond the scope of this book. Instead, I recommend Simon Wardley's original blog series.[3]

Tech Trends and Your Customer's Market

The third section of the O&O artifact addresses your customer's market and relevant technological trends that could impact their business and products.

If your customer is the company that makes potato peelers, this section might describe:

- *Market trends:* Is there an increased demand for pre-peeled potatoes or other vegetables? Are there new cooking trends influencing how people prepare food?

- *Competition:* What other companies offer similar products or services? How do they position themselves in the market? Are there new players who could challenge the traditional potato peeler?

- *Technological trends:* Could new technologies like automation, artificial intelligence, or sensors be used to develop more efficient and user-friendly potato peelers? Are there other technologies that could change how people prepare food at home?

By carefully analyzing these factors, you might better understand how your customer—the potato peeler manufacturer—might change their products in the future and, consequently, their needs as your customer.

Opportunities and Outcomes Inspire Your OKRs

The fourth and fifth sections of the O&O describe the customer's opportunities and outcomes. In this part of the artifact, it becomes more concrete how the O&O serves as a basis for creating guiding star OKRs. It's quite common for a guiding star objective (the "O" in an OKR) to be closely aligned with the customer outcome described in the fifth section of the O&O. The customer opportunities you gather in the fourth section can also inspire variables that work well as the guiding star's key results (the "KR" in an OKR), as shown in the image on page 39.

---

3.   https://medium.com/wardleymaps/on-being-lost-2ef5f05eb1ec

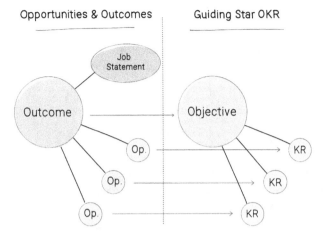

To identify "opportunities" for Beza Trucks, Trusted Tools focuses on the truck manufacturer's challenges and frustrations. Trusted Tools collects negative quotes that highlight obstacles, annoyances, and workarounds in Beza's current processes. Examples of such quotes could be:

- "It's difficult to get an overview of all assembly data."
- "We lose time manually double-checking each bolt."
- "It's cumbersome to share assembly data with other departments."
- "We have trouble identifying sources of error in production."
- "Our current system isn't flexible enough to handle changes in production pace."

The reason why these annoyances should inspire your key results—not your objectives—is that you're not looking for things to fix in your current product but for more general quality checks for objectives that empower the customer with new capabilities.

Conversion from opportunities to key results is sometimes straightforward:

- *Opportunity:* "We lose time manually double-checking each bolt."
- *Key result:* Number of bolts manually double-checked per week: from X to 0.

The final section of the O&O, as mentioned earlier, describes the customer's potential outcomes. Here, you paint a picture of their ideal scenario. Imagine how their daily life could be improved if the problems and obstacles you identified no longer existed. What new opportunities would this open up for them? Focus on the customer's experience and describe this future vision freely, without limiting yourself to specific formats or product solutions.

Converting an outcome to an objective makes it more tangible. For example, the industrial tool developer Trusted Tools could use the outcome "Increased productivity and efficiency in engine assembly" to create the objective "Engine assembly is streamlined, with minimal wasted time and resources."

This objective focuses on a more specific, targeted future. It remains tied to the selected outcome by describing how the company will achieve it.

Key Takeaways

- By understanding your customers' ecosystem, you can create products that not only meet their needs but also exceed their expectations with innovative solutions.

- The Opportunities and Outcomes artifact is a central resource, used in the catchball process and highlighting your customers' real needs, goals, value chain, market landscape, and relevant technological trends.

- Instead of focusing on product features, understanding your customers' jobs-to-be-done helps you grasp their true motivations and desired outcomes.

- Analyzing your customer's value chain through Wardley mapping reveals how different components of their offerings evolve and relate to each other, uncovering opportunities for innovation.

- By examining technological trends and your customer's market landscape, you can anticipate future changes and adapt your products accordingly.

- Identifying your customers' pain points and challenges can lead to the development of key results that measure progress towards eliminating those problems.

- Describing the desired future state for your customers, free from the limitations of existing problems, helps you set ambitious yet achievable guiding star objectives.

What's Next?

Now that you've explored how to create an O&O artifact and discover your guiding stars, prepare to learn about the catchball process, a vital tool for creating shared goals and ensuring everyone in the organization is involved and engaged.

Catchball: Defining Guiding Stars Cross-Collaboratively

Catchball—inspired by the Japanese strategic planning framework *Hoshin Kanri [CD97]*—offers a collaborative approach to setting organizational goals within the Guiding Star OKR framework. This structured process encourages a dynamic exchange of ideas, ensuring everyone contributes to shaping the organization's direction. By promoting inclusivity and moving away from traditional top-down directives, catchball aligns with modern leadership styles and fosters a more engaging goal-setting process.

In this chapter, we'll explore how catchball operates across all levels of an organization, breaking down hierarchical barriers. We'll also examine the connection between catchball and the influential work of management theorist Mary Parker Follett, whose ideas on collaborative leadership continue to resonate in modern organizations.

Additionally, we'll introduce the OODA concept and its connection to catchball, demonstrating why involving all perspectives speeds up decision-making and improves your goal accuracy.

Finally, we'll discuss cadence and horizon in setting goals at different levels, and how shared OKRs and strategy broadcasts can foster shared purpose and drive collaborative work.

A Collaborative Exercise

Imagine having a Sunday picnic with good friends. After eating, you start tossing a tennis ball around. It's fun and challenging, with no winners or losers.

An old man strolls by and observes the ball moving faster and faster between you. Your goal is to maintain this momentum, fostering a flow of ideas and energy. This is the essence of catchball—a collaborative exercise in which everyone's unique perspectives combine to create something extraordinary.

Let's take a look at an example of how the catchball process can work in a four-level organization: CTO, portfolio owners, project managers/product managers, and development teams (see also the image on page 43).

1. *The CTO initiates.*

    The CTO begins by creating drafts of one to three guiding star OKRs and presents them to the portfolio owners in personal meetings.

2. *The CTO asks for feedback and reflection.*

    The CTO asks the portfolio owners to consider two questions:

    (a) "Are these OKRs understandable to you?"

    (b) "Are these the right OKRs, or should they be adjusted?"

3. *The portfolio owners give feedback.*

    The portfolio owners take the questions home, reflect, and then return with feedback to the CTO.

4. *The CTO adjusts (if necessary).*

    Based on the feedback, the CTO adjusts the OKR drafts.

5. *The ball is passed on.*

    Now it's the portfolio owners' turn to create one to three OKR drafts at their level and ask their product and project managers to review these OKRs based on the same two questions (a) and (b) in step 2. The portfolio owners also seek feedback from the CTO to ensure that knowledge from both top-down and bottom-up perspectives is incorporated.

6. *The process continues.*

    Catchball continues down and up the organization. Product and project managers have their OKRs reviewed by the development teams and the portfolio owner while the development teams have their goals reviewed by the product and project managers.

7. *Conduct a strategy broadcast.*

    After defining all OKRs, you conduct a company-wide strategy broadcast to ensure that everyone understands and aligns with the current long-term goals.

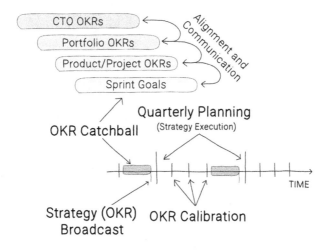

The entire process precedes the agile planning and usually takes two weeks. Keep a high pace, but don't underestimate the required time. There's a deadline but no strict schedule for each step. The ball flies back and forth through the air, and no one counts the number of throws. It's important to remember that feedback can be just as valuable for higher levels since the information might reveal areas where they need to adjust their goals or strategies.

Not all OKRs are created equal. Some are "inspired guiding stars," aligning directly with higher-level goals. Others are "local," for example, focusing on specific products, such as improving a music app's recommendation algorithm—a goal not directly relevant to the CTO's overarching vision.

The image on page 44 illustrates a company's portfolio of smart home products, focusing on security and thermostat devices. Two teams contributing are the camera team and the door lock team. Arrows indicate that a guiding star is "inspired" by another guiding star at the level above it. Those without upward arrows are instead "local."

Remember, an "inspired" guiding star isn't merely a subset of a higher-level goal—it's a unique strategic objective that creates viable value while still supporting the bigger picture. Treating OKRs like projects or task lists that can be broken down into sub-projects or sub-tasks is sometimes referred to as "cascading OKRs"—a term derived from the Italian word for "waterfall." That top-down approach isn't suitable for the dynamic nature of strategic goals. I strongly advise against cascading OKRs.

The beauty of catchball isn't about who has the final say, but rather the collaborative exchange of ideas and knowledge as drafts are reviewed throughout the organization. This back-and-forth creates a synthesis, blending insights

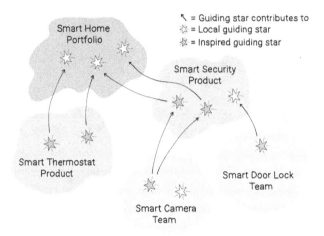

from every level to shape the most effective OKRs. No one "owns" the process or has the "best" ideas—it's about using collective intelligence to find the best direction. Like cooking a delicious dish, each unique ingredient contributes to the final result, making it difficult to pinpoint the origin of any single flavor.

In the previous example, the CTO, portfolio owners, and others assume the OKR-initiating role of *guiding star sponsor*—a hat they then wear throughout the lifecycle of a guiding star OKR. But true innovation often stems from collective intelligence. Consider assembling a diverse group of experts when brainstorming your initial OKRs. This cross-functional collaboration often leads to more holistic perspectives, minimizing biases and blind spots. It's just one example of how emergent collaboration within the Guiding Star OKR framework can spark ideas no single individual could've conceived on their own.

Catchball is a structured process of informal, organic conversations, *not* debates or large group votes. The latter often results in either the most pow-erful person—not necessarily the most knowledgeable—getting their way or a mediocre compromise. It's also *not* about mechanically breaking down large projects into tiny, non-viable pieces that can then be handed off to separate teams to work on in isolation.

Why Hierarchy Still Matters (Even if You Hate It)

Top-down goal setting is rarely successful, but completely abandoning hierarchy isn't ideal either. Fortunately, there are ways to integrate decision-making across a large organization, as Mary Parker Follett suggested (see *Mary Parker Follett Didn't Like Compromises*).

In a small family, it's often easy to keep track of everyone's needs and wishes. You can easily communicate and make decisions together without any formal structure. But imagine the family lives in a big city with many other relatives and a great number of extended family members. Suddenly, it becomes much more difficult to coordinate everyone's needs and wishes. It becomes chaos without an overarching structure to organize and govern the city, with different levels of focus and decision-making.

Similarly, small companies can function without explicit hierarchies, as everyone knows each other and collaborates easily. But as companies grow and become more complex, structure becomes essential for aligning efforts toward common long-term goals and ensuring efficient and effective decision-making.

Hierarchy in the Guiding Star OKR framework isn't about power dynamics but rather about creating a clear structure for managing your complex reality. Different levels focus on different aspects of the business, from strategic planning at the management level to specialized tech expertise at the team level.

Like a small company, effective information flow is crucial for any organization, regardless of size. Formal structures alone aren't enough. Frequent, informal interactions across levels are necessary to avoid bureaucracy and maintain agility. Cross-pollination (see Chapter 7, Cross-Pollination: Everyone's Ears, Insights, and Ideas, on page 79), calibration (see Chapter 6, Calibration: Fine-Tuning Guiding Stars, on page 65), and catchball make the Guiding Star OKR framework an antidote to the hidden chaos of unchecked bureaucracy.

Mary Parker Follett Didn't Like Compromises

Mary Parker Follett [Ton03] was a pioneering thinker in management and organizational theory during the early 1900s. Her ideas were revolutionary for that time and are still relevant today.

One of Follett's most famous stories involves two people in a library who disagreed about an open window. One person felt hot, while the other feared catching a cold. Instead of a half-open compromise, they found a solution benefiting both: opening a window in an adjacent room.

The story illustrates Follett's view of conflicts and the advantages of integration over compromise. A compromise means that both parties give up something, which often leads to no one being completely satisfied. Integration, on the other hand, is about finding a solution where all needs are fully met, as with the window.

The catchball process emphasizes collaborative conversations to determine what the organization can truly accomplish rather than competing for project funding.

Big OODA Is the Secret to Faster and Better Goals

John Boyd, [Cor04] a brilliant military strategist, realized that success in combat wasn't only about superior firepower but also about making faster, better decisions than the enemy. He described this human information process as the Observe, Orient, Decide, Act (OODA) loop:

- *O—Observe:* Gather information about the situation.
- *O—Orient:* Analyze the information and understand what it means.
- *D—Decide:* Choose the best course of action.
- *A—Act:* Implement the plan.

The faster you complete this loop, the greater your advantage. It's similar to making two chess moves while your opponent makes one. Our brains, composed of billions of specialized neurons, collectively observe, orient, decide, and act, forming a sophisticated system for processing information and making decisions.

Similarly, a company can be seen as a large brain, where each employee is a neuron with unique knowledge and experience. By including everyone in the OODA loop—that is, the big OODA—you can leverage collective intelligence to make faster and more accurate decisions.

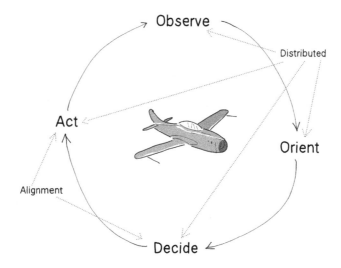

The big OODA provides the conditions for everyone to participate in every step of the loop:

- *Everyone observes.* By involving employees at all levels, you get a broader picture of the situation and can detect changes and opportunities earlier.

- *Everyone orients.* Different perspectives and experiences help you interpret the information in a more nuanced way and avoid blind spots.

- *Everyone decides.* By giving employees the opportunity to influence decisions, you increase their commitment and motivation while taking advantage of their knowledge and creativity.

- *Everyone acts.* When everyone is involved in the decision-making process, it becomes easier to implement changes quickly and efficiently.

The OODA image highlights "Decide" and "Act" as being in "Alignment." This emphasizes how catchball, pupation, calibration, and cross-pollination foster both rapid, decentralized decision-making and the ability to take swift, localized action—all while remaining in sync with the overall strategic direction.

The image also emphasizes "Distributed" in all four steps. Distributed decision-making is the opposite of centralized decision-making—think micromanagement—but it's also different from delegation. Delegation simply transfers authority from one person to another, often requiring the delegate to report back and get approval.

Consider these two examples to understand the difference:

Distributed

Schools of herring move synchronously and change direction with lightning speed. They have no leader who decides, but each fish observes its neighbors and adjusts its movement accordingly. This distributed decision-making makes it difficult for predators to catch individual fish.

Delegated

In baboon troops, a hierarchy exists with a dominant male at the top. He makes the overall decisions but often delegates tasks to other males in the troop, such as patrolling the territory.

The individual herring makes decisions based on a common goal: not to become dinner for a predator. But no top boss decides who is in charge of what as is the case with the baboons.

Distributed decision-making isn't a universal solution, but under the right circumstances, it has advantages like more engagement, better solutions, and faster results over time. But it can lead to groupthink. Delegation frees up leaders' time and develops employees, but it risks bias and uninformed choices.

The best companies know when to use each approach—distributed, delegated, or centralized—for optimal results.

Catchball is a prime example of accelerating the company's big OODA loop. While it may seem resource-intensive, my experience shows that catchball expedites decision-making, leading to better guiding stars faster. By ensuring everyone is informed and contributing their unique expertise, the big OODA minimizes rework and missed opportunities, ultimately saving the organization valuable time. Additionally, it fosters ownership and commitment among colleagues who actively participate in the process.

The Role of the Guiding Star Sponsor

In the previous example of a four-level organization, we saw that guiding stars could be initiated by various roles: the CTO, portfolio owners, product managers, project managers, and even development teams. The principles of catchball remain effective regardless of the specific number of levels within your organization. The common thread among these initiators is that they all assume the role of the guiding star sponsor. This isn't a full-time position, but rather a responsibility that individuals take on during the lifecycle of a guiding star—whenever it's relevant.

The Guiding Star OKR framework emphasizes a collaborative and decentralized approach to goal-setting and execution. This implies shared ownership and responsibility, although certain areas of responsibility are associated with the guiding star sponsor.

The spark that ignites a guiding star
> The sponsor proposes the guiding star during the catchball process, typically after collaborating with a cross-functional team to brainstorm a long-term sustainable goal.

The navigator who guides the direction
> The sponsor actively participates in strategy broadcasts, calibration sessions, and other relevant meetings. They serve as the central point of contact for any questions about the guiding star's purpose and implications, ensuring clarity and alignment even in informal settings.

The committed observer
> The sponsor maintains an active interest in the progress made toward the guiding star, staying informed and offering guidance when necessary.

The sponsor's role specifically excludes:

- *Project Management:* The sponsor isn't responsible for the day-to-day management or execution of tasks related to the guiding star.

- *Ultimate Accountability:* While deeply involved, the sponsor doesn't bear sole responsibility for the guiding star's success. The entire team shares this responsibility.

The guiding star sponsor shares leadership responsibilities with the guiding star liaison, a role that will be explored further in Chapter 5, Pupation: Integrating Guiding Stars with Agile Planning, on page 55.

OKR Leadership

by: Joakim Manding Holm, Organizational Coach, Adaptiv

At one challenger bank, they were keen to try OKRs. The IT leadership team seemed to enjoy setting goals. I guess the more traditional managers liked the feeling of control it gave them.

The more progressive members of the team had another reason. They believed that goal-setting was important because that was the only way a modern manager could guide an organization forward. "Set goals, then leave the teams alone," they said.

At face value, this may sound great—a modern leadership approach. In reality, it resulted in absent leaders doing "management by numbers," reviewing only the results of the OKRs once per quarter.

This hands-off approach also signaled to the development teams that this OKR thing maybe wasn't that important after all, making correct prioritization a challenge. I learned then that without continuous attention from leaders, for example, by coaching teams on continuous improvement through experimentation, it's hard to succeed with OKRs.

Different Levels May Have Different Cadences

As in nature, different levels in an organization have different rhythms and speeds. Compare how atoms vibrate at a furious pace, while the larger molecules they form move much more slowly. Similarly, a development team in a company can set new goals every other week—sprint goals in a scrum team—while a CTO might establish new objectives annually.

The table shown in the illustration on page 50 offers a fictional example of the varying cadences at different organizational levels.

The higher up in the hierarchy you go, the more extensive and complex the decisions become. A CTO needs to consider a variety of factors, such as market trends, competitive situations, and long-term goals before the CTO can set the direction for the entire company. It takes longer to collect and analyze all relevant information at that level, and the decisions might have greater consequences.

Higher levels in the organization must remain agile and adaptable to respond to external changes. This means that while calibration is crucial at all levels,

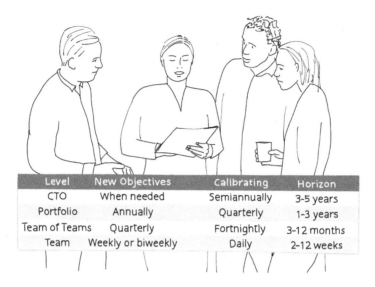

Level	New Objectives	Calibrating	Horizon
CTO	When needed	Semiannually	3-5 years
Portfolio	Annually	Quarterly	1-3 years
Team of Teams	Quarterly	Fortnightly	3-12 months
Team	Weekly or biweekly	Daily	2-12 weeks

guiding stars at higher levels should avoid excessive details since such details are more likely to require adjustments.

The four-level example on page 43 illustrated the activities within the organization during a catchball process in preparation for quarterly planning. The table in this section indicates that compared to the quarterly cadence of the team of teams, the development teams have a higher cadence (one to two weeks), while the portfolio and CTO have a lower one. How does this work together?

To ensure that quarterly guiding stars at the team of teams level are feasible, each development team starts by drafting all their own two-week goals for the whole quarter. These shorter-term goals, in scrum called "sprint goals," outline the team's objectives for their own iterations (or sprints). Think of these drafts as flexible plans—not promises—subject to change throughout the quarter.

Each team's goal is formally agreed upon during the team's iteration planning (sprint planning) session. That is, the team's goal for the upcoming two-week iteration is defined immediately before that period starts. Before this planning session, the team's goal sponsor (often the product owner in a scrum setting) prepares a goal proposal for the team, based on three key factors:

- The initial draft, created during the team of teams' quarterly planning.
- Insights gained from various team of teams calibration sessions.
- New information and learnings that have emerged since the initial draft.

A few days before the team's planning session, the team's goal sponsor and representatives for the relevant team of teams (like product or project managers) discuss the proposed goal. This ensures alignment and shared understanding across different levels, rather than a top-down mandate.

This collaborative approach works well beyond the scrum framework. Whether your team uses iterations or a more fluid workflow, regularly revisiting and refining goals through collaborative discussions leads to better outcomes.

The team's goal sponsor has the flexibility to propose a "local goal" for the team (see local and inspired guiding stars on page 44). This means a goal that might not directly contribute to any higher-level guiding star but still holds significant importance for the development team's vision.

Furthermore, at the team level, calibration often takes the form of the less formal daily sync-up, which some teams call the "standup" and others the "daily scrum" or the "daily pulse."

The higher levels maintain their slower cadence and thus participate actively in the catchball for the team of teams, even though they themselves are unlikely to create new guiding stars at their levels. You might recall that guiding star sponsors at all levels are both navigators and committed observers.

It's important to distinguish between cadence—how often goals are set—and target horizon—how far into the future goals extend. A CTO can set goals with a multi-year horizon, even if those goals are updated annually. Guiding stars focus on transformative leaps. Dedicated effort toward a goal this year can create momentum that propels the organization forward, even if the goal itself is no longer your guiding star at the highest level next year.

Shared OKRs Drive Collaborative Work

Sharing OKRs can be an effective way to promote collaboration and create a sense of shared responsibility within an organization. Let's say two product managers, Alice and Bob, work with a different team of teams within the same organization. Both teams are working to make it easier for new users of a specific product to quickly do advanced things. So Alice and Bob have a common objective:

- *Objective:* Advanced features quickly become understandable for new users of Product X.

Shared OKRs are a powerful tool for providing a consistent user experience across products, preserving the conceptual integrity of architecture across teams, ensuring consistent technology usage throughout the organization, and doing much more.

Sometimes, it may be enough that the direction (the objective in an OKR) is the same, even though the property metrics (the key results in an OKR) differ. This gives each team the flexibility to tailor their efforts to their specific circumstances while working toward a common goal. It's important to remember that not all OKRs need to be shared and that each team should have its own unique goals based on its specific role and responsibilities.

Strategy Broadcast Provides Clarity and Participation

A week before the agile quarterly planning, it's time for the strategy broadcast—the final step in Catchball where you share the selected guiding star OKRs with the entire organization, ensuring everyone is aligned and understands the strategic direction.

How you conduct strategy broadcasts can vary. It doesn't have to be a big meeting for all levels at the same time. The important thing is to include three key elements:

- *Clear communication of guiding stars:* Present which guiding stars apply for the coming quarter. Also, justify why you've chosen these particular guiding stars and which ones you've rejected.

- *Open dialogue and questions:* Invite everyone to a lean coffee[1] session in which they can ask questions and discuss what the goals mean for their particular role and team. It's okay if not all questions can be answered immediately. For example, an unexpected question that perhaps no one can answer right away could be, "How will the new goal affect our collaboration with external partners?"

- *Transparency and documentation:* Make sure that all guiding stars are documented in a single location to which everyone has access. This creates transparency and ensures that everyone knows what applies even after the strategy is broadcast.

In addition, for each guiding star, a *guiding star liaison* is also nominated—a catalytic role that differs from a traditional project manager. While project managers typically focus on managing budgets, adhering to timelines, and ensuring deliverables meet quality standards, the liaison's primary responsibility is fostering the generation and dissemination of knowledge and insights

---

1.   https://leancoffee.org

among the various teams, experts, and stakeholders involved. After the strategy broadcast, the liaison's first task is to identify and connect these groups, creating a virtual and collaborative "team of teams." Chapter 5, Pupation: Integrating Guiding Stars with Agile Planning, on page 55, will provide a more comprehensive exploration of the role of the guiding star liaison.

The strategy broadcast is where your guiding stars truly come to life, evolving beyond the words in your objectives and key results. It's during this broadcast that a shared understanding of your direction and trust in that vision truly crystallizes. In addition to the OKR, the guiding star encompasses this collective consciousness, acting as a catalyst for collaboration, engagement, and collective intelligence. These positive outcomes are then further amplified through the processes of calibration and cross-pollination.

By clearly communicating the goals and allowing room for lean coffee discussions, you create this common understanding of the direction you intend to move and why this is important. Moreover, when employees are given the opportunity to ask questions and discuss the goals, they feel more involved and motivated to contribute. The open dialogue also allows you to identify potential challenges and obstacles early in the process and deal with them proactively.

By conducting catchball and strategy broadcast well before the agile quarterly planning, teams and managers can align their work with the guiding stars in the pupation process. This ensures that strategically important tasks, crucial for achieving long-term goals, are prioritized alongside urgent tasks—that is, in the same single backlog—preventing them from being constantly sidelined.

Strategy broadcast is a powerful tool for creating clarity, commitment, and participation in the company's strategic direction. Think of this event as a necessary part of the catchball process and so as a contribution to the big OODA—that everyone observes, orients, decides, and acts.

Key Takeaways

- Catchball is a collaborative process in which everyone's unique perspectives are valued. It aims to create a flow of ideas and energy throughout the organization.

- The process of defining OKRs isn't a one-time event. It's an ongoing conversation, where feedback and adjustments are encouraged at all levels.

- Hierarchy is important for aligning a complex organization toward common goals. Different levels focus on different aspects, ensuring effective decision-making.

- Involving everyone in the Observe, Orient, Decide, Act loop (big OODA) harnesses collective intelligence for quicker, more accurate decisions.

- Different levels in the organization have different rhythms and speeds when setting and adjusting goals.

- Sharing OKRs encourages teams to work together toward common objectives, fostering a sense of shared responsibility.

- A well-conducted strategy broadcast ensures that everyone understands the selected guiding star OKRs and their rationale, creating clarity and commitment.

What's Next?

Now that you've seen how to collaboratively define guiding stars, in the next chapter, you'll learn how to integrate them into execution planning, ensuring strategic work isn't forgotten in daily tasks.

Pupation: Integrating Guiding Stars with Agile Planning

In the fast-paced world of agile product development, it can be challenging to find a balance between delivering quickly and working toward your long-term goals. It's easy to get caught up in day-to-day work and lose sight of the big picture.

In this chapter, we'll explore how to integrate guiding stars into the agile planning process so that your work contributes to the company's long-term objectives without compromising the flexibility and adaptability that agile methods offer.

By bringing together strategic goals and tactical execution, we create an environment in which each agile iteration moves us closer to the future we want to create. It's not about abandoning agile principles but about giving them a clear direction and purpose. Let's explore how to do this in a way that strengthens both the team's motivation and the company's long-term success.

The Essential Period Between Caterpillar and Chrysalis

The period that begins with the strategy broadcast and ends with the planning of the next agile iteration—for example, quarterly planning—is sometimes called *pupation*, as it's as vulnerable and crucial as the transition of the caterpillar into a chrysalis in the life cycle of a butterfly.

The caterpillar's main goal is to eat, grow, and store energy. This is similar to the catchball process (see Chapter 4, Catchball: Defining Guiding Stars Cross-Collaboratively, on page 41), where the initial ideas from the discovery process (see Chapter 3, Discovering Customer Opportunities, on page 29) are refined into inspiring visions—the guiding star OKRs.

The chrysalis, on the other hand, doesn't consume anything. It's a haven where the adult structures of the butterfly are developed, fueled by the energy stored during the caterpillar stage. The chrysalis stage mirrors the focused period—the iteration or timebox—in which teams develop new things.

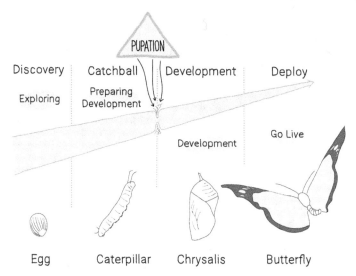

In nature, parasites, predators, and extreme temperatures can disrupt a butterfly's pupation—the delicate shift from caterpillar to chrysalis. You can prevent similar disruptions by taking crucial pupation steps between the strategy broadcast and agile planning. These steps will ensure that your guiding star doesn't stagnate or eventually die but instead transforms into a focused chrysalis and eventually a vibrant, resilient butterfly that goes live one day.

The three key steps in the pupation phase between strategy broadcast and agile planning are:

1. *Identify the team of teams.*

    Immediately after the strategy broadcast, the *guiding star liaison* figures out what experts, teams, and other relevant people are needed to begin moving toward the guiding star. They come together to form the initial team of teams. This group is virtual, meaning its members bring work back to their regular teams. As you learn more, the composition of the team of teams may change. It's important to confirm that these are the right people but not to get bogged down in discussions about their availability. Remember, guiding stars are a priority.

2. *Brainstorm viable results.*

   Whether your upcoming agile iteration planning is focused on a few weeks or the next quarter, the guiding star's horizon may be further out. So, think about what's a reasonable outcome within this upcoming iteration. Guiding stars aren't projects with milestones. Instead, think that when this timebox is over, there should be something viable that provides feedback for the next timebox. The journey becomes self-sustaining; seeing progress fuels your motivation.

3. *Formulate development tasks.*

   In *The Mythical Man-Month: Essays on Software Engineering [Bro95]*, Frederick P. Brooks Jr. wrote, "For the human makers of things, the incompletenesses and inconsistencies of our ideas become clear only during implementation." When you start developing, the only thing that's certain is that along the way, you'll probably adjust your perception of what you should do to achieve the viable results you brainstormed in step 2. That's not failure—it's learning. Create a plan based on your best understanding right now, and be ready to adapt.

Example: Trusted Tools in Pupation

You may remember the company Trusted Tools in Chapter 3, Discovering Customer Opportunities, on page 29. They established the following key result:

- Number of bolts manually double-checked per week: from X to 0

Here's an illustration of what the three steps in the pupation process might look like:

1. *Identify the team of teams.*

   The guiding star liaison identifies and assembles a cross-functional and virtual team of teams. It includes quality assurance, assembly line teams from the customer (Beza Trucks) and possibly engineering teams that designed the assembly process or tools involved.

2. *Brainstorm viable results.*

   The team of teams brainstorms ways to reduce manual double-checking. They might consider the following:

   - Implementing error-proofing mechanisms in the assembly process to prevent incorrect bolt installations in the first place

   - Introducing real-time sensor technology that verifies proper torque and automatically logs data

> • Adding visual or auditory cues to the assembly tools to confirm proper bolt installation

3. *Formulate development tasks.*

    The team of teams outlines specific tasks to implement the selected solutions. The plan might include the following:

    > • Designing and testing new fail-safe mechanisms
    >
    > • Researching and selecting appropriate sensor technology
    >
    > • Modifying existing tools or developing new ones with integrated feedback systems

The focus is on creating a solution that eliminates, not just reduces, the need for manual double-checking. The team's efforts during this timebox should result in a tangible improvement, even if the ultimate goal of zero double checks isn't fully achievable within this time frame.

I want to emphasize that step 3 only "outlines" these tasks, not "defines" them. This is an initial draft from the team-of-teams to prepare for the official quarterly planning session. These proposals will be reviewed and refined when a larger group of stakeholders participates in the integrated planning process. The goal is to arrive at that session with a shared and well-developed plan.

Balancing Important and Urgent in the Plan

The third step in pupation (formulate development tasks) generates candidates for the next development timebox—the next iteration. In agile planning, these items are then prioritized alongside other tasks that may be more urgent but not as crucial for the organization's long-term goals.

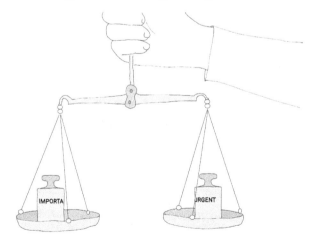

Urgent development tasks that are already underway have clear next steps. Don't reverse-engineer guiding stars for them, as that's unnecessary and counterproductive. It's best to incorporate them into the plan as they are.

The ideal outcome of the planning process is a balanced mix of urgent and important tasks. But if the three pupation steps aren't completed for your guiding stars before planning begins, it's highly unlikely that any progress will be made in their direction.

Agile Planning: Balancing Adaptability and Focus

The term *agile* has been interpreted in many ways since Steven L. Goldman and his colleagues explored it in the early 1990s (see *Agile Competitors and Virtual Organizations: Strategies for Enriching the Customer [GNP94]*). In the years since, many—though not all—have come to associate *agile* in part with a rhythmic approach to organizing work that's particularly well-suited to fast-paced environments such as product development.

Rather than creating a rigid, up-front plan for an entire project, agile planning focuses on assigning a small portion of work to an upcoming timebox. This way of working is both iterative and incremental:

- *Iterative:* The same plan–do–check–act (PDCA) process is structuring each timebox.
- *Incremental:* At least once during the timebox, viable results are ready for delivery—without the need for project milestones or tollgates.

The length of a timebox can vary, with shorter intervals bringing teams closer to continuous agility. But overly short intervals can disrupt the focus necessary for successful delivery.

The book you're holding contains numerous examples of quarterly planning cycles for team of teams, supplemented by weekly or fortnightly planning within individual teams. While the Guiding Star OKR framework is agnostic about the length of these planning cycles, it does emphasize the importance of balancing short-term agility with long-term goals in these planning sessions.

Agile planning techniques can never be an excuse to neglect broader goals. Instead, the ideal agile plan should encompass both urgent, near-term tasks and development initiatives that contribute to the company's overarching strategic direction as defined through the collaborative catchball process.

The Role of the Guiding Star Liaison

In Chapter 4, Catchball: Defining Guiding Stars Cross-Collaboratively, on page 41, you learned how the catchball process culminates in a strategy broadcast, an essential step in ensuring that everyone in the organization understands the guiding stars you've chosen. During or before the strategy broadcast, a guiding star liaison is appointed for each guiding star. Unlike a traditional project manager, who focuses on deliverables, budgets, and time-lines, the liaison's role is to facilitate the generation and sharing of knowledge across different teams, experts, and stakeholders. Although the liaison shares leadership responsibilities with the guiding star sponsor (the role that we explored in Chapter 4, Catchball: Defining Guiding Stars Cross-Collaboratively, on page 41), they are two distinct roles that are interdependent and can only succeed or fail together.

Think of the liaison as a catalyst in a chemical reaction. A catalyst facilitates a reaction without being consumed. Similarly, the liaison facilitates collaboration and knowledge exchange without taking ownership of the work itself. The liaison's role isn't about being the source of all knowledge—it's about fostering an environment where insights and ideas can flow freely, enabling the team of teams to reach its full potential. The liaison might achieve this by facilitating workshops, helping teams establish clear communication channels, or ensuring everyone has access to the same information in a centralized system. The liaison may also play a crucial part in aligning the team's efforts and ensuring everyone is moving in the same direction.

Ultimately, each individual team is responsible for continuously collaborating across team boundaries and driving the work forward, even without a liaison. The liaison's role is to connect, empower, and enable, not to become a permanent bottleneck or an excuse to delay decisions and actions.

During pupation, the liaison plays a vital role in holding the team of teams together so that it can complete the three steps. This begins immediately after the strategy broadcast, when the liaison identifies and connects these groups, creating the virtual team of teams that will work together in the second and third pupation steps to move the company toward the guiding star. The goal is to provide the upcoming agile planning with concrete input from this guiding star in the form of epics, backlog items, use cases, or however you define your development tasks.

The liaison also remains important even after agile planning, when the actual development work is underway. They can facilitate cross-pollination (see Chapter 7, Cross-Pollination: Everyone's Ears, Insights, and Ideas, on page 79) and calibration (see Chapter 6, Calibration: Fine-Tuning Guiding Stars, on page 65) sessions, but that's not a requirement. At this stage, the liaison also regularly assesses whether the right teams, experts, and stakeholders are included in the team of teams, adding or removing members as needed to ensure that the development work proceeds as smoothly and efficiently as possible.

Most importantly, the liaison must be able to foster collaboration and knowledge sharing so that you can collectively reach your guiding stars.

Liaison Can Be a Career Opportunity

A liaison is skilled at facilitating events and has a deep understanding of the areas touched by this guiding star. They could be a business manager with keen insights into customer needs, a team coach experienced in fostering collaboration, an architect who understands the technical challenges, or someone else.

The liaison role is more like a temporary hat that someone wears than a static position. This gives more people the opportunity to grow and contribute. Managers, human resources (HR) personnel, and others who influence career paths should encourage people to take on the liaison hat—it's a valuable growth opportunity.

The Team of Teams

In General Stanley McChrystal's book *Team of Teams: New Rules of Engagement for a Complex World [McC15]*, "team of teams" refers to a military organizational model in which traditional hierarchies and departments are replaced by networks of smaller, autonomous teams. These teams share a common purpose, openly share information, and work closely together to solve complex problems. The goal is to create an organization that's more adaptive, responsive, and efficient than traditional structures, as shown in the image on page 62.

In the business world, the team of teams is a pivotal element in realizing your guiding stars. It's a dynamic network of experts, development teams, and other stakeholders united by a common goal: propelling the organization toward its long-term vision.

Members contribute their unique skills and perspectives while remaining part of their regular teams. The actual development work—prioritized through agile planning—takes place within these individual teams. The shared

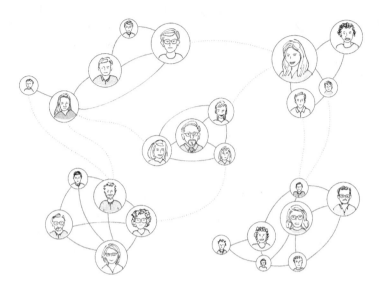

responsibility of the team of teams is to ensure that the combined result of all teams is aligned and creates viable customer value.

This network of teams is flexible, adapting as you learn and as new needs arise. You may need to add expertise in a specific area or involve a new stakeholder group. This flexibility allows you to leverage all the knowledge and insights available within the organization. The guiding star liaison is responsible for keeping track of who's in and who's out at any given time.

The team of teams is active in pupation, calibration, and cross-pollination. It helps turn guiding stars into concrete development steps, evaluate progress, adjust key results, and share insights that lead to new opportunities.

Collaboration and knowledge sharing are at the heart of the team of teams. By working together, sharing ideas, and learning from each other, you can overcome obstacles, find innovative solutions, and create the synergy needed to move toward your guiding stars.

Always Maintain a Unified Task List

Many organizations struggle to make room for proactive work. Urgent tasks often end up in a separate backlog from long-term ones, creating conflicting priorities. When this happens, urgent tasks have a disproportionate advantage over important long-term goals.

To counteract this, your teams should maintain their single, unified task list. This list should include everything from urgent tasks to those that will get you closer to your long-term goals, even if they're not pressing right now. By prioritizing everything together in the same planning process, you ensure that the strategy has a direct impact on day-to-day work.

Of course, you still need flexibility for unplanned incidents and catastrophic issues. It's all about finding a balance between delivering quickly, working toward long-term goals, and having the flexibility to deal with the unexpected.

By integrating strategic initiatives directly into your work planning rather than leaving them on the sidelines, you create a culture where long-term goals are always present. This enables you to make decisions that not only solve today's problems but also bring you closer to the future you want to create.

Key Takeaways

- The pupation phase between strategy broadcast and agile planning is critical for translating guiding stars into actionable steps. The three key steps in this phase are identifying the team of teams, brainstorming viable results within the upcoming timebox, and formulating development tasks.

- Agile planning should balance urgent near-term tasks with development initiatives that contribute to long-term strategic goals. It's crucial to maintain a unified task list that encompasses both, ensuring that the strategy directly influences your daily work.

- The guiding star liaison acts as a facilitator, fostering collaboration and knowledge sharing among the team of teams. Their role is crucial in ensuring successful pupation and ongoing development work.

- The liaison's role extends beyond pupation, facilitating cross-pollination and calibration sessions and ensuring that the right people are involved in the team of teams. The liaison helps maintain alignment and momentum throughout the development process.

- The team of teams is a dynamic network of experts, development teams, and stakeholders working together to achieve the guiding star. They contribute their unique skills and perspectives while remaining embedded within their regular teams.

- The team of teams is essential for calibration and cross-pollination, helping to refine key results, share insights, and uncover new opportunities. Collaboration and knowledge sharing are at the heart of their effectiveness.

- Flexibility and adaptability are key throughout the process, as the composition of the team of teams and its development tasks may evolve based on new learnings and needs. The focus remains on making tangible progress toward the guiding star, even if the ultimate goal isn't fully achieved within a single timebox.

What's Next?

Planning alone won't guarantee the success of guiding stars. The next two chapters will teach you how to adapt to new insights and a changing environment, which are crucial for keeping your strategy relevant. First, you'll learn how to fine-tune guiding stars in calibration sessions and then how to share insights during cross-pollination.

CHAPTER 6

Calibration: Fine-Tuning Guiding Stars

Calibration is an essential tool for fine-tuning the direction you've previously set for your guiding stars and for boosting both your colleagues' intrinsic motivation and their alignment.

Imagine you're hiking in the woods. Even though you've already set a course, a small mountain or stream may prevent you from taking the shortest route. The detours around the obstacles put you off course. So you need to take out your map, compass, GPS, or any navigation equipment you have to see if you need to adjust your direction. These moments are like the guiding stars' calibration sessions.

Remember, you're looking to the future, not at who has done what up to now, and how what has happened matches historical plans. No medals are awarded, and no reprimands are given during calibration. This forward-looking principle makes the calibration session format different from a project follow-up meeting, and it doesn't resemble a traditional OKR check-in either.

In this chapter, you'll learn how to facilitate calibration sessions that encourage collaborative decision-making, promote strategic focus and alignment, and enhance intrinsic motivation within the teams.

Calibration as an OODA Loop

Remember the OODA loop from Chapter 4, Catchball: Defining Guiding Stars Cross-Collaboratively, on page 41? It's a simple but powerful decision-making model: observe, gather information about the situation; orient, understand what that information means; decide on the best course of action; and act to implement your decision. This Observe, Orient, Decide, Act cycle—or OODA loop—was developed by military strategist *John Boyd,* *[Cor04]* and it reflects how most of us naturally process information and make choices in our daily lives.

The calibration session participants, as a group, engage in OODA loops, which unfolds as follows:

1. You share new *observations.*

2. You *orient* yourselves to where you are, whether you're moving, how fast you're moving, and in what direction you're moving.

3. You may make *decisions* to calibrate your direction.

4. You *act* by documenting changes and informing the organization.

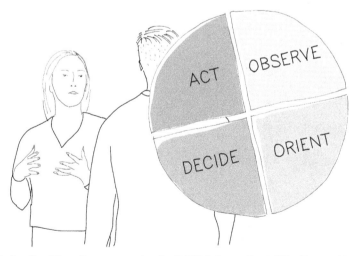

Don't think of calibration as a single OODA loop that fills the entire session. Instead, hundreds or thousands of loops are started and finished during the session. These loops might trigger each other, overlap, or otherwise last for a short or long time. What all the loops have in common is that they're based on the OODA principle.

The complexity in your organization—for example, the vast amount of formal and informal interactions between colleagues every day—makes it impossible to micromanage the entire company top-down, even if you wanted to for some strange reason. You need everyone's eyes, everyone's experiences, and everyone's good ideas to make your collective performance as good as possible.

The final adjustment decisions are made by the respective guiding star sponsor, but of course, this doesn't contradict the fact that you strive for a broad analysis during the session and a broad dissemination of information afterward. The calibration sessions are open and inclusive. Everyone is welcome. The meeting invitation isn't limited to certain people, and all the decisions you make are documented openly.

Components of Calibration

The calibration typically lasts 55 minutes, and you have five items on the agenda:

1. *Set the Scene.* The facilitator reminds the participants of your current guiding stars' overall purpose—this might be as short as one to five sentences—and then shares external news highlights. This entire point should take a maximum of 5 minutes, so prepare it carefully.

2. *Weather Report.* Broadcasters share your current state, direction, and speed of motion. This may sometimes be conducted by the facilitator and prepared by broadcasters.

3. *Orientation.* The facilitator leads a lean coffee[1] session with the broadcasters and the expert-or-curious. Orientation fills 50–75% of the calibration time.

4. *Forecast.* Broadcasters briefly discuss whether they're considering adjusting their respective guiding stars. But they make the formal decision and inform the organization (*broadcast*) the next working day to allow time for a slow, deliberate, and effortful type of thinking.

5. *Closing.* The facilitator informs everyone about the date for the next calibration.

---

1. https://leancoffee.org

Let's take a look at the three roles mentioned in the agenda:

- *Facilitator.* This individual reminds everyone of these particular guiding stars' overall purpose, shares external news, and facilitates the whole session. Since the facilitator doesn't necessarily need to have a stake in the outcome, anyone can take on this role. The important thing is the person is skilled at facilitating and is preferably knowledgeable about the area the guiding stars touch upon. It might be a project manager, an agile coach, a scrum master, or someone else.

- *Broadcasters.* Typically, these are the guiding star liaison. They prepare and may present the weather reports, participate in the orientation, and share their views on the forecast.

- *Expert-or-curious (EoC).* They listen to the introduction, the weather report, and the forecast. They participate in the orientation. They might be customers, stakeholders, engineers, business experts, or other product team members.

A more detailed example with tips for how to facilitate the event can be found in Facilitating a Calibration Session, on page 72.

How Many Guiding Stars Should Be Included?

You want to keep meetings to a minimum, so sometimes, you'll cover multiple guiding stars in a single session. Calibrations are designed to fit within 60 minutes, ideally 55 minutes, to give everyone a breather before their next meeting. It's crucial to finish on time. That's why you need to strike a balance when deciding how many guiding stars to include in the session.

If you combine multiple guiding stars in one session, the key is choosing the ones that make sense together. Avoid automatically grouping guiding stars simply because they share a sponsor or liaison, or even because they impact the same portfolio. That prioritizes efficiency but not necessarily value.

Instead, think from the customer's perspective: Which guiding stars would the same customer groups be interested in? If discussing those together attracts colleagues from across the company, that's a win. This means that you're breaking down silos and focusing on what truly matters. The goal is to facilitate discussions that are relevant and valuable to the attendees, regardless of their level, role, or association with the guiding stars being discussed.

How Often Should Calibration Occur?

The frequency of calibration depends entirely on your organization's needs. A good starting point is to hold calibrations three times per iteration: after 20%, 40%, and 60% of the iteration time. You might notice that these aren't evenly spaced over the whole iteration since there's no calibration during the last 40%. There's a reason for that.

Projects often need a last burst of energy near the end for a successful delivery. But remember, guiding stars aren't about project delivery; they're about your long-term direction. In strategy, there's no such thing as "near the end."

For example, let's say 75% of the iteration time has passed. You've either made rapid progress toward your guiding star or your advancement was minimal to nonexistent. In either case, guiding stars aren't the right tool for a last-minute push. Prioritizing the completion of an outdated plan isn't a recipe for success. Especially not when it comes to strategic work.

Moreover, on the development team level, which is below the team of teams level, calibration often manifests as the less structured daily sync-up, commonly called a "standup" or "daily scrum."

How to Adjust a Guiding Star

The calibration session may result in an urge to adjust one or more guiding stars. You may then use refactoring, preserve optionality, or raise the horizon—three different approaches—to make these adjustments.

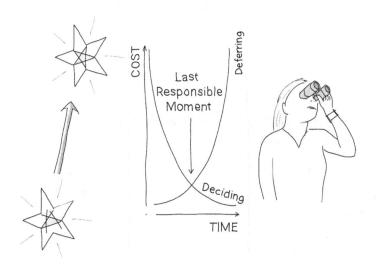

Refactoring

> This is a popular method in agile software development. The developer restructures an existing body of code, altering its internal structure without changing its external behavior. When you refactor a guiding star, you reformulate or perhaps replace some key results but only to avoid misunderstandings. It points in the same direction as before but with a better explanation.

Preserve optionality

> You may keep some options flexible for as long as it's responsible to do so. For example, you decided to go on a vacation to Paris and book flights or train tickets. But you're not deciding which hotel to stay in until you've asked friends about their experiences from previous trips to Paris. The equivalent in calibration is to specify details that you intentionally left open at the start of this guiding star iteration. See Mary and Tom Poppendieck's *Lean Software Development [PP03]* for details about the *last responsible moment.*

Raising the horizon

> If you're already close to or have even passed what your guiding star described at the start of the iteration, you may raise the horizon further. This method is also useful when you feel there is too much focus on how and not enough focus on why—further horizon often clarifies the purpose. If the horizon was previously one year, you might instead consider where you want to be in two years' time. Remember that since guiding stars are forward-looking only, the end of the iteration and the horizon aren't the same thing. For example, during the coming year, you may work in a direction toward a guiding star that describes where you want to be in two years' time. In this example, the iteration ends in one year, and the horizon is two years away. Zooming in on binoculars brings your more distant future into sharp focus.

The following examples illustrate each method, using the guiding star from the tax authority as a basis:

- *Objective:* Easy for me as a citizen to file my taxes.

- *Key result 1:* Average time to complete a digital tax return: from X minutes to Y minutes.

- *Key result 2:* Number of incorrect tax returns: from X to Y.

1. *Refactoring:* Change key result 1 to "Average user satisfaction rating for the digital tax return process: from X to Y," to better capture the subjective experience of ease.

2. *Preserve optionality:* If the initial OKR didn't specify the types of tax returns included, decide during calibration to focus specifically on income tax returns for individuals.

3. *Raising the horizon:* If significant progress has been made on simplifying the tax filing process, expand the objective to include not only filing but also understanding tax regulations, with new key results reflecting this broader goal.

From a purely technical point of view, adjustments to guiding stars naturally mean changing, removing, or adding objectives or key results. Here are three ways to do this:

1. *Add, remove, or reword key results.* Key results are concrete and quantitative examples of what things might look like once your objectives are met. Don't forget that achieving all key results doesn't prove that the objectives have been met.

2. *Fine-tune the objectives.* It's uncommon to adjust objectives, but sometimes you want to clarify what you mean. Clarifying might be part of your prior tactic to intentionally keep options open. You may also need to clarify when you notice that many people misunderstand the intent of the current wording.

3. *Remove or add new OKRs.* When you're completely convinced that a guiding star points in the wrong direction, you should remove it. This is a major intervention in your strategy and should only be used in emergencies. One of the most important components of strategic execution is persistence. Remember the beaver colony mentioned in Balancing the Trifecta of Strategic Execution, on page xiv.

A rule of thumb is that every time you add something during your calibrations, you remove another thing of at least the same magnitude. Too many concurrent goals nullify their ability to function as a strategy. Plus, removing one thing doesn't necessarily mean that you have to add another. An example is when someone starts a prioritization discussion during a calibration session. That kind of discussion should be a no-no. Don't prioritize strategies against each other; choose them or choose not to have them. Instead of prioritizing A against B, remove either A or B. This helps clear the doubt about what is most important.

Facilitating a Calibration Session

Besides preparing and following up, calibration consists of five parts within the session itself. To ensure a smooth session and maximize the return on your time investment, you need to consider several factors.

Preparation

Broadcasters do more than share updates on key results. They also need to gather feedback on how the objectives are being understood across the organization. This information should be sent to the facilitator beforehand, regardless of who's presenting during the calibration. Questions that may be answered:

- Is the guiding star properly understood by the organization?
- Did this guiding star influence planning in execution?
- Is there new progress that might be interesting to others?

Set the Scene

This first part of the session is typically run by the facilitator and should never take more than 5 minutes. The purpose of "Set the Scene" is to frame the context and share any news that might impact the guiding stars. Begin by briefly reminding everyone about the overall purpose of these guiding stars. You may then, for example, share new insights from market research or data analytics.

Weather Report

In the second part of the session, you assess where you stand and how you're moving toward your guiding stars. The reports are prepared beforehand and are either presented by the facilitator or the broadcasters. This may include, but isn't limited to:

- Remind everyone about the whys.

- Align the big picture: where you are, whether you're moving, how fast you're moving, and in what direction you're moving.

- Inform about what's coming up.

Orientation

The third part of the session is where you delve into the unknown, taking up at least 50% of the calibration session. The two earlier parts gave you a high-level overview, but it's in orientation that you can uncover unwanted tipping points before they become major problems. Using a lean coffee format, you create an emerging agenda and novel discussions across teams that might never happen otherwise.

This is how to run the orientation in a lean coffee format:

- *Gather topics:* People write discussion topics on sticky notes.

- *Vote:* Everyone gets a few dot votes to mark their most interesting topics.

- *Prioritize:* Highest-voted topics form a backlog for discussion.

- *Timeboxed discussions:* Set a short timer (5–8 minutes) for each topic, encouraging focused conversations.

- *Move on:* When the timer ends, move to the next topic, or decide if more time is needed.

Forecast

The last 5 minutes, the fourth part, of the session are for reasoning and speculation from your guiding star sponsors. What speaks for an adjustment of this guiding star, and what speaks against it? What might an adjustment look like? Is it a refactoring, a limitation in alternatives, or should you raise the horizon?

The guiding star sponsor won't make the decision about adjustment until the following day. This creates space for careful analysis and consideration of long-term consequences, and it helps avoid errors caused by impulsive, emotional responses. Daniel Kahneman coined the term *System 2 thinking* to capture this, in contrast to *System 1 thinking* during the calibration session, which might be fast, automatic, and effortless. See Daniel Kahneman's *Thinking, Fast and Slow [Kah13]* for details.

Closing

In the fifth part of the session, the facilitator informs everyone about the date for the next calibration.

Broadcast

The guiding star sponsor or liaison updates their OKRs in a single location accessible to everyone— fostering transparency—by the next workday. This is essential for

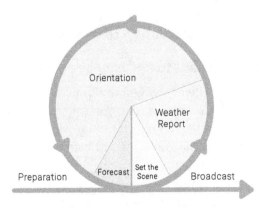

maintaining clarity and alignment across your teams, so there are no exceptions to this rule. Avoid using personal slides or other presentations, as they create confusion and undermine trust. Everyone needs to see the same decisions to work effectively.

Strategy Drives Execution

The calibration session isn't about the executable tasks (sometimes called features, epics, stories,[2] or something similar) you've derived or will derive from your guiding stars. You certainly have other meetings for that in your execution framework. A guiding star sponsor can still send signals that have a good chance of influencing future work. Each adjustment of a guiding star may impact how much time and energy people spend on different tasks. The following image visualizes an example of how this may be structured.

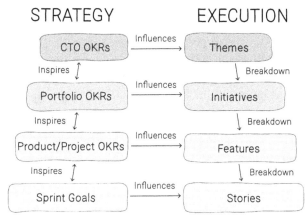

Compare this to the decision-making meetings of the central bank's Federal Open Market Committee (FOMC) when setting the U.S. federal funds rate. The FOMC knows that its decisions have a major impact, especially in the medium term. But the only thing it decides on is the interest rate, not what others should do as a consequence of the changed interest rate.

Focus Leads to Persistence and Alignment

It's a challenge to ignore the pressure to start even more projects, both from within the organization and from your environment. Regardless of how stormy it's outside, it's important that you allow the organization to focus consistently on the same guiding stars before you consider changing direction. Strategic execution is, by definition, proactive, not reactive.

---

2.   https://www.atlassian.com/agile/project-management/epics-stories-themes

Organizational focus—having fewer goals overall—makes it easier to maintain a consistent direction long enough to see the impact of your work. This also creates a more fertile ground for alignment.

Persistence

Many people have an interest in adding more guiding stars. Two examples are the project manager who is on the final stretch before a major customer delivery but can't find personnel with key skills and another project manager who has been waiting a long time for his project launch to get approval. They each may see a new guiding star as ensuring they get the support they need. A third example is the product manager who has discovered promising new product ideas, perhaps even backed up by solid research data. And a fourth example is the salesperson who claims to be inches away from a new huge contract if only you implement a few new features. However, "The urgent is not important, and the important is never urgent," as Dwight Eisenhower said.[3] In calibration, you couldn't care less about how urgent matters may seem. Your strategic focus is on what contributes to your long-term goals.

Alignment

Let's say you're buying a new smartphone, and you're considering two popular models: A and B. The specifications and prices don't differ much between A and B. You ask some friends, and coincidentally, both happen to be owners of A who say they're satisfied with their purchases. So you buy A. Economist Brian Arthur[4] called this phenomenon increasing returns and noted that now one more person—that is, you—recommends A. Collectively analyzing and possibly calibrating the chosen guiding stars puts them on top of many people's minds. As more of you prioritize these particular goals rather than other goals, you also spread the energy organically, even to those who weren't at the session.

If there's pressure to drastically change your guiding stars during calibration, it's everyone's responsibility to consider whether those changes can wait until the next guiding star iteration begins with its new catchball process.

Calibration Fuels Intrinsic Motivation

Before a calibration session, a participant tells you that she's nervous because she worries that her achievements haven't been good enough. This is a sign

---

3. https://quoteinvestigator.com/2014/05/09/urgent
4. https://sites.santafe.edu/~wbarthur

that the session is focusing on the wrong things. Calibration shouldn't be about performance measurement.

Intrinsic motivation—the joy of doing something simply because it's enjoyable or fulfilling in itself—comes from things like autonomy, mastery, purpose, growth, and social interactions. Especially when it comes to knowledge work and long-term vision, intrinsic motivation trumps extrinsic motivation—carrots and sticks. It's another reason to encourage broad participation, a reflective session, and a long-term focus in your calibration sessions.

It's worth acknowledging that your organization may have performance-based incentives in place. But it's essential that these incentives aren't linked to your guiding star OKRs in any way. The potential consequences of mixing incentives with guiding stars are complex and beyond the scope of this discussion, but suffice it to say that such a practice is strongly discouraged.

It's natural for teams to object to frequent or drastic changes in direction. They may have built their quarterly plans around the initial guiding stars, expecting to see results later on. If you change things too often, they might lose faith in the process, making it harder to gain traction with future guiding stars.

Remember, everyone's perspective is shaped by their unique experiences. When you forget that, it's easy to dismiss objections as "resistance to change" instead of trying to see things from their viewpoint.

Building trust takes time and effort, but it can be lost in an instant. Let's focus on understanding your teams' concerns and working together to find the best path forward.

The Complementary Puzzle Piece: The Cross-Pollination

Calibration is where you make formal decisions, with everyone hearing the same information. But sometimes, you might have a valuable detail that's not relevant to the whole group or want to share a new idea without derailing the session. Maybe you have a question that feels trivial but is important to you. That's understandable, as everyone plays a different role in calibration.

That's why calibration works hand-in-hand with another important piece—cross-pollination—which is the theme for the next chapter. There, you learn about how to foster open discussions and knowledge-sharing. Together, calibration and cross-pollinations create a result that's more powerful than either could be alone.

Key Takeaways

- Calibration is a fine-tuning tool, not a performance review. It's about adjusting direction for guiding stars, boosting motivation, and increasing the alignment of the organization.

- Think navigation, not project follow-up. Calibration looks forward to achieving a long-term strategy rather than dwelling on what's already happened.

- The OODA loop is the foundation. Calibration helps you observe, orient, decide, and act continuously in a strategic context.

- Distributed decision-making is key. Everyone's perspective matters for success. Calibration is inclusive, encouraging open discussion and information-sharing.

- Strategic focus and alignment drive results. Calibration helps you avoid getting sidetracked so that you can achieve your most important goals and work with a sense of unity.

- Adapt thoughtfully, not radically. Constant change undermines trust and focus. When major guiding star changes are truly necessary, consider refactoring, preserving optionality, or raising the horizon.

- Calibration fuels intrinsic motivation. Focusing on long-term goals, collaborative decision-making, and a sense of purpose boosts morale and commitment organically.

What's Next?

The next chapter describes calibration's companion: cross-pollination. Neither works without the other. Cross-pollination is a concrete method for fostering collaboration and knowledge sharing between teams, leading to shared understanding, new insights, and better decisions.

CHAPTER 7

Cross-Pollination: Everyone's Ears, Insights, and Ideas

Cross-pollination is the necessary companion of the calibration session (see Chapter 6, Calibration: Fine-Tuning Guiding Stars, on page 65). Cross-pollination makes the Guiding Star OKR framework fluid, natural, and life-like. During this session, novel ideas emerge and are quickly adopted by the organization, with the strengthening of your informal network being a valuable side effect.

In this chapter, you'll discover how the cross-pollination session is structured and why it's essential for strategic execution. You'll also understand how cross-pollination differs from calibration, encourages the concept of quenched disorder, and fosters intrinsic motivation within your team.

Embrace Quenched Disorder

Imagine two chocolate bars that look identical at first glance. Although both are delicious, dissimilar manufacturing processes hide differences inside the bars.

In the first chocolate bar, the ingredients were carefully mixed and then cooled slowly, allowing air bubbles and unevenness to disperse evenly. The result is a bar with a smooth and pleasant texture.

The second bar was hastily mixed together by an impatient chef. The mixture was cooled immediately, trapping air bubbles and unevenness. The result was a chocolate bar with an uneven and unexpected disorder—a surprise in every bite.

Now imagine you run a business and want your strategy to lead to tangible results. You have defined clear strategic guidelines and have regular calibration sessions. But despite this, you find that the strategy isn't reaching its full potential. Why? Part of the problem may be the lack of *quenched disorder* in your organization's ways of working. To understand why quenched disorder is so important, let's first delve into the concept.

Quenched disorder is a phenomenon borrowed from physics that describes what happens when a material is cooled very rapidly. This rapid cooling creates a random disorder in its crystal structure. In an organizational context, we can see quenched disorder when we orchestrate impromptu encounters between diverse and exceptional colleagues. Novel ideas and innovation are born in this ambiguous environment. This is different from formal meetings with fixed agendas and established roles.

If the chocolate bar with rapid cooling is quenched disorder, then the slowly cooled one is annealed disorder. In a meeting with an annealed disorder, we decide in advance what we'll talk about, who the expert is on what, and what we'll decide on. And so it turns out that we go through what we think is important together and then make decisions in a structured way. These types of meetings are necessary and valuable—no doubt about that. But they need to be complemented by quenched disorder meetings, at least if we want unexpected encounters, collective intelligence, and innovation.

In the Guiding Star OKR framework, the calibration session represents annealing, while cross-pollination takes care of the need for quenching. The combination of calibration and cross-pollination is a delicious two-course meal.

What Is Cross-Pollination?

Let's take a look at an example. Cross-pollination is an event that happens every Friday for all employees of the company—regardless of organizational level, area of expertise, or job description. The session always starts at nine o'clock and is no longer than 55 minutes. The format is inspired by Open Space Technology (OST), a self-organizing session in which participants create and manage the agenda around a central theme or question in real time.

In cross-pollination, participants spontaneously decide at the last minute what topics will be discussed. This means that conversations may vary from time to time. The only common property of all topics is that they have a connection to your current guiding stars.

Parallel discussions take place in several different rooms. Each room is dedicated to a unique topic. Participants decide which discussion they want to participate in. Plus, if, during the discussion in one room, they notice that they're neither learning anything nor contributing, they can leave that room for one of the other rooms. The latter is called "the law of mobility" in OST.

Cross-pollination also emphasizes two principles from OST as outlined in Harrison Owen's *Open Space Technology: A User's Guide [Owe97]*:

- "Whoever comes is the right people." (Everyone is welcome and appreciated.)

- "Whatever happens is the only thing that could have [happened]." (The freedom to explore a topic.)

A more detailed example with tips for the person facilitating the event and sending out the invitation can be found in Facilitating a Cross-Pollination Session, on page 87.

Agila Sverige's Minimalist Recipe for Success
by: Ola Ellnestam, Software Coach, Agical

"Let's do a conference!" "A conference?" "Yes, wouldn't it be cool to have a local Agile conference that reinforces the Swedish community?"

"You're crazy!" "How are we going to manage that?" "We're only a handful of people who see one another regularly."

"I think I know how we can spread the work, reduce risks, and increase the commitment."

"How?"

"The conference format will be Lightning Talks[1] and Open Space."

This is pretty much how the conversation went when an industry colleague of mine pitched the idea of a Swedish Agile conference. In the end, the proposal turned out to be exactly what we needed to dare to try organizing our own conference.

Therefore, three months later, we completed the first edition of Agila Sverige (Agile Sweden).[2]

Over two days, 150 people gathered and talked about Agile. That was three times as many participants as we originally thought.

Before lunch, we were inspired by lightning talks, and in the afternoons we talked in Open Space sessions. By the end of the conference, we had listened to 40 lightning talks and had chosen roughly the same number of Open Space sessions.

Today, almost twenty years later, the conference still runs annually. Using the same format: Lightning talks and Open Space Technology. I believe that this is the key to the success of Agila Sverige. Its permissive format allows and encourages grassroots involvement, which in turn gives the conference its unique sense of participation and an inclusive atmosphere.

Cross-Pollination Is as Necessary as Calibration

Cross-pollination sessions are as necessary as calibration sessions for several reasons:

Stimulates unexpected encounters
    Since participants spontaneously choose topics, cross-pollination breaks down hierarchies and silos. You get new connections and unexpected encounters between ideas and people.

Freedom to explore
    The freedom to delve into issues that are currently engaging participants leads to creative dialogs and new perspectives that you might never have seen in a more structured environment.

---

1.   https://www.forbes.com/2010/01/14/presentations-pecha-kucha-technology-breakthroughs-oreilly.html

2.   https://agilasverige.se

Quick response to new challenges

The flexibility of choosing discussion topics in cross-pollination enables the organization to quickly respond to new challenges and opportunities in a changing world.

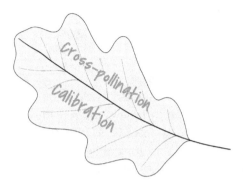

It's impossible to overstate how important cross-pollination is for making strategic execution the transformation engine you all hope for. The effects of cross-pollination that I've personally observed vary between companies and industries, but they're always just as amazing:

Intrinsic motivation

Both the employee's engagement and their intrinsic drive increase when they have the opportunity to actively participate in discussions about the current guiding stars. Purpose, growth, and social interactions are important factors in creating intrinsic motivation. You'll get a more dedicated and productive workforce.

Increased innovation

When insights and perspectives from different levels and teams meet, that leads to unexpected connections, new perspectives, and creative solutions that no one could have come up with on their own. It's like seeds from different plants are combined to create new, unique, and stronger plants.

Broader perspective

Cross-pollination gathers insights and ideas from across the organization. It provides a more nuanced and broader picture of the challenges and opportunities in working toward the guiding stars.

Improved communication

In addition to documented decisions made in formal forums, a modern organization wants many small insights to be spread efficiently, be borderless, and be individually adapted. The same specific detailed information is vital for some and, at the same time, annoying noise for many others. The dialogue that arises in small, mixed sessions will automatically be about what's relevant to those who are talking to each other.

Continuous alignment

Open communication between levels, departments, and teams in cross-pollination helps you to continuously agree on your latest insights and understanding of everything that you associate with your current guiding stars.

Faster decision-making processes

Although cross-pollination itself isn't a decision-making meeting, participants will leave the session with new concrete ideas and discover potential issues that might otherwise have been missed or uncovered later. These findings are crucial inputs for formal decision-making meetings, helping the organization make quick, well-informed decisions about strategy execution.

Strategy focus

The lifeblood of a strategy is that it's top of mind for many of your colleagues. If everyone is working on different—admittedly interesting and valuable—things, then what you have is organizational multitasking, not an executed strategy. Recent thoughts and conversations have a greater chance of popping up again than older ones. The high frequency (weekly) of cross-pollination reminds everyone of which guiding stars they're working toward right now.

Strengthens the informal networks

By talking to and about trusted people, early humans were able to build cooperation on a larger and larger scale (see *Sapiens: A Brief History of Humankind [Har15]* by Yuval N. Harari). This resulted in adaptability and the development of complex organizations, which are important aspects, even in today's business world. Let's examine that scaffolding mechanism further.

Scaffolding with Informal Networks

Formal structures and hierarchies are common in any organization, but so are informal networks of relationships between employees. Informal networks cannot be designed. They're built on trust. We turn to the person we trust when we need extra expertise or brainpower to succeed in our work.

The more diversified your informal network is, the greater the chance that you'll have access to the right type of capability you need in a specific situation. Cross-pollination helps to create that diversity for you.

If you trust Alice, and Alice trusts Bob, then maybe you trust Bob too—perhaps not as much as you trust Alice though. The further away you are—one step to Alice, two steps to Bob—the less you trust a colleague. This is precisely what researchers Duncan Watts and Steven Strogatz investigated in *Six Degrees: The Science of a Connected Age [Wat04]*. Their results were clear and remarkable.

In the following illustration, graph A on the left shows 20 people (dots) who each trust (link with) their four closest neighbors. The average distance of trust between two randomly chosen people is almost three steps in this graph. Unfortunately, your level of trust isn't always that high for your friend's friend's friend.

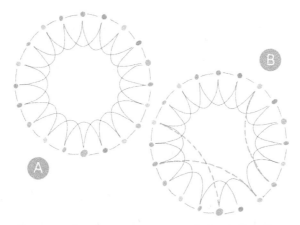

What happens if we randomly rewire some of the links, for example, as the dotted lines in graph B on the right? This is where it gets spectacular. On average, the first five random changes of links in this model will *halve* the average trust distance between two randomly selected employees. Once a distant connection, this person has become someone you know and trust, and you believe that trust is mutual. Wiring new trusted connections across is the holy grail for boosting efficiency in large-scale collaboration.

Does this only apply to a group of 20 people? Not at all. This heuristic is true regardless of the size of the network. Imagine what five new trust links in a company of 1000 people would do!

The number five is, of course, not magical. My point is that the suddenly emerging conversations in cross-pollination—about things we are passionate about—build trust for colleagues at other levels and in other parts of your organization.

The shortcuts built into the informal networks create an effective scaffolding structure. In this structure, information travels faster and finds the right person more easily—every day! The company can adapt better and more quickly to all types of change.

Autocatalysis—If We Have It in Us, It Will Emerge

If you reflect on your company's past successes and their contributing factors, you might agree that some of those factors could have been seemingly random coincidences that unexpectedly played a significant role. Perhaps it was a spontaneous discussion during lunch, a failed experiment that gave surprising insights, or a new employee who questioned what you had always done. Cross-pollination creates new connections and pathways (shown in the following image as dotted lines), distinct from the formal organizational structure (solid lines). These seemingly random interactions significantly increase the likelihood of those critical, game-changing moments occurring within the company.

Autocatalysis is a fascinating phenomenon in which the product of a chemical reaction also acts as a catalyst for that same reaction—that is, the product speeds up the very reaction that created it. You get an avalanche effect of increased production.

The origin of life—one of the most crucial yet challenging scientific questions—might be explained by autocatalysis, a process where a collection of simple molecules evolved into the complex, self-sustaining forms we now recognize as living organisms. (see *Complexity: The Emerging Science at the Edge of Order And Chaos [Wal92]* and *Autocatalytic Sets: From the Origin of Life to the Economy [Hor13]*)

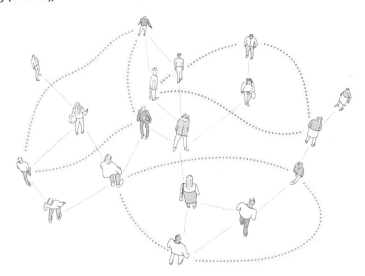

In a figurative sense, you get autocatalysis when your employees interact across borders and silos in cross-pollination sessions. They collaborate, share ideas, and learn from each other across organizational levels and team boundaries. The learnings create new opportunities for learning, and the effect is a positive chain reaction of innovation and productivity.

Facilitating a Cross-Pollination Session

Cross-pollination consists of five parts, in addition to preparation. Here are some tips on how to facilitate.

Preparation

Firstly, you ensure you've prepared all the tools needed during the session. For each discussion room, you need a separate place and something to collaboratively draw on. If you're meeting in person, you may place chairs in circles with a flip chart next to each circle. For a digital remote session, you create links to breakout rooms with digital whiteboards.

You also have a central location where you can gather at the beginning and then later reassemble. There, you prepare a whiteboard or something similar to a matrix for the agenda. The matrix has two rows, one for each discussion session, and it has as many columns as there are discussion rooms. Above each column is the name or ID number of a discussion room. In the second part of the session—"Create Agenda"—you'll write a topic in each cell. See the example of an agenda matrix on page 88.

Each cross-pollination starts with a lightning talk, a concise presentation format designed to quickly convey a specific idea or topic to an audience. You maintain a buffer of at least three upcoming lightning talks. This means that you've booked speakers for specific dates and agreed on topics.

Send out the invitation well before the first session. A template for what it could look like can be found in the sidebar, Here's What an Invitation Might Look Like, on page 89.

Set the Scene

The purpose of this first part of the session is to create inspiration before the discussions. You do that by kicking off the cross-pollination with a five-minute lightning talk—that is, a short, deep dive into something.

The dive might, for example, be into market information from a salesperson, a technical solution described by one of the engineers, or shared knowledge from a subject-matter expert about their domain. Anything connected to your guiding stars goes.

If the lightning talk hasn't finished after five minutes, it will be interrupted by a sound signal, and everyone will applaud. There's no room for exceptions here.

Create an Agenda

In the second part of the session, the participants collaboratively build the agenda and you facilitate that process. Ask the room directly for topics that relate to your current guiding stars. That will make the participants suggest topics spontaneously. Capture keywords or very short phrases from what they say and write the names of the topics in the matrix—one row for each timebox, one column for each discussion room, and one topic for each cell.

Try to create a sense that there's not much at stake here; the names of the topics don't need to be perfect. Rather, the titles are preferably a little bit ambiguous. This avoids unnecessary constraints on your creativity. You honor the OST principle: "Whatever happens is the only thing that could have." The name of the topic is only a starting point—which direction the discussion will take is up to those who choose that discussion room.

Avoid any topic titles that sound like decision points, for example, "Decide on a technical solution." Other meetings exist for that.

Sometimes someone suggests that people may email topics in advance, or even that a jury should select the best topics. Don't go there! You already have plenty of these types of meetings. Remember, one of the purposes of cross-pollination is to generate novel ideas and innovation through quenched disorder—by creating unexpected and unprepared interactions between smart, highly educated people.

Don't spend more than five minutes creating the agenda—ideally less.

Discussion Sessions

The third and fourth parts of the session are two rounds of discussions. Regardless of when they start, end the first round 30 minutes into the session and the second one 50 minutes into the session.

Participants choose which discussion room they want to be in and have the privilege of changing rooms when they feel they aren't learning or contributing—the law of mobility. Don't see this as criticism of anyone.

The topic that the room received from the agenda is a starting point, and the direction of the discussion is up to the participants.

Closing

This is when you thank everyone and provide information on when the next cross-pollination session will take place. That was the fifth part of the session.

Here's What an Invitation Might Look Like

Subject: Join the Discussion! Cross-Pollination This Friday

Hi [Name],

This Friday, we're hosting another round of cross-pollination, a forum for all employees to share ideas and collaborate across teams and levels.

Why you should join:

- Spark your creativity: Dive into discussions on our guiding stars with colleagues from different areas. You might gain unexpected insights or discover new ways to contribute.

- Boost your impact: Learn from others and share your expertise. Together, we can accelerate progress on our guiding stars.

Why it matters:

- Cross-pollination is crucial for fostering innovation and breaking down silos. Your participation is key to building a more collaborative and successful organization.

Details:

- When: Friday, [Time]
- Where: [Location] (or link for virtual meeting)
- Topic: We'll brainstorm topics together at the start!

See you there!

Best,

The Cross-Pollination Team

There Are No Formal Meeting Notes in Cross-Pollination

Always remember the importance of quenched disorder in cross-pollination sessions. The value of these sessions lies in their spontaneity and the unexpected interactions they foster. If documenting every insight would have been a mandatory practice, the sessions risk transforming into structured, formal meetings that stifle creativity and discourage open dialogue. The focus would shift from exploration and idea generation to note-taking and information capture.

The essence of cross-pollination is to embrace the unpredictable and allow for the emergence of novel ideas. By engaging in documentation, you risk losing the serendipitous connections and insights that arise from unplanned conversations and free-flowing discussions. The pressure to record everything can inhibit participants from sharing their thoughts openly, fearing judgment or scrutiny. The emphasis on documentation could also lead to a more passive participation style, where attendees focus on capturing information rather than actively engaging in the conversation.

In essence, the value of cross-pollination lies in its ability to break down barriers, encourage open dialogue, and foster an environment where unexpected ideas can flourish. While taking personal informal notes is perfectly acceptable, the focus in cross-pollination sessions shouldn't be to generate documentation.

Key Takeaways

- Cross-pollination sessions are essential for successful strategy execution, alongside calibration sessions. They bring fresh perspectives and unexpected connections that lead to innovation and faster responses to challenges.

- Cross-pollination sessions are inspired by Open Space Technology (OST). Topics are decided on the spot, participants can move freely between discussions, and creativity is encouraged.

- Cross-pollination fosters "quenched disorder," a way to help unexpected innovations emerge. This is crucial because planned meetings (annealed disorder) might miss valuable ideas that arise from spontaneous interactions.

- The benefits of cross-pollination for employees include increased engagement, intrinsic motivation, and the chance to learn from diverse colleagues.

- Cross-pollination strengthens informal networks within the organization. By connecting with colleagues from different departments, employees build trust and improve future information flow.

- Cross-pollination optimally leads to autocatalysis, a positive feedback loop in which innovation breeds more innovation. Collaboration across teams and levels sparks new ideas and solutions.

- Cross-pollination sessions are designed to be low-pressure and engaging. Participants can choose topics and leave discussions that aren't relevant to them.

What's Next?

Having explored discovery, catchball, integration with agile planning, calibration, and cross-pollination—guiding stars in action—you're now ready to explore additional concepts beyond the core process. Part III of this book will unveil seven fundamental principles for crafting a strategy. This part also includes a guide on how to implement this framework step-by-step, and it highlights potential challenges to be aware of. By the end of Part III, you'll have a comprehensive understanding of how to leverage the power of the Guiding Star OKR framework.

Part III

Succeeding with Guiding Stars

We have now arrived at the final part of the book. In the first two parts, we covered both the theory and practice of the Guiding Star OKR framework. Now it's time to take a step back and look at seven overarching strategy principles and how to successfully implement the framework in your own organization. I hope this third part will give you further insights and inspiration to create a culture of persistence, alignment, and adaptivity when striving toward long-term goals. Let's dive in!

CHAPTER 8

Seven Principles of Good Strategy

Congratulations on making it this far! I didn't doubt for a second that you would. You're now equipped with the knowledge and tools to embark on your own guiding star OKR journey.

In Part I of this book, we covered the fundamentals of OKR: objectives and key results. In Part II, we explored the processes necessary for successfully implementing the Guiding Star OKR framework in your organization. We covered everything from discovering customer opportunities to integrating guiding stars into your agile planning process.

But why stop there? Just as a skilled chef doesn't rely solely on a recipe but understands the underlying principles of cooking, mastering guiding star OKRs requires grasping the core principles that drive their effectiveness. These principles are the secret sauce that will elevate your OKR game from good to outstanding. So, let's dive into these seven principles and uncover the essence of what makes a good strategy.

Principle 1: Craft a Common Direction

Your current products are successful, and you're making a profit. You address regulatory requirements, match competitor features, and keep the lights on. So why invest in long-term strategies?

Consider your brain: billions of neurons, each with its own task, create connections and networks. They achieve incredible things without central control. You can learn languages, play instruments, solve problems, create art, and innovate if you have a direction.

The iconic opera virtuoso Montserrat Caballé probably didn't practice bending free kicks, and the superstar soccer player David Beckham probably didn't try opera. They dedicated their entire lives to honing their craft in one specific direction. Do you want to play guitar or paint? Choose one, even if both are enjoyable. The more of your time your brain concentrates on one sole craft, the better you'll become at it.

A company is similar. It's made up of individuals with unique roles and expertise. These individuals collaborate, interact, share information, and solve problems. Like neurons, they achieve more together than any individual is capable of—but only with a common direction.

To evolve, a company needs a strategic direction that harnesses the collective energy of its employees. Without this shared focus, the organization risks stagnating, missing opportunities, and falling behind competitors. By facilitating a dynamic exchange of ideas and insights across all levels of the company, the catchball process ensures that the guiding star OKRs you define are relevant and meaningful to everyone involved. Furthermore, through ongoing cross-pollination, the understanding of your chosen direction is continually refined and aligned, fostering a unified sense of purpose and direction throughout the organization.

Principle 2: Discover Transformative Leaps

A strategy is often defined as a plan to achieve long-term goals. We choose the most important goals and allocate resources accordingly. But, because the world is constantly changing, it might be better to describe a direction rather than fixate on a goal. We want to go "that way" (in that direction), not "there" (to that place). We want to head south, not necessarily exactly to Marrakech (as shown in the image on page 97).

Here are some concrete examples of guiding star objectives:

- Medtech: Malaria is eradicated.
- Banking: Minimal intervention is needed in my everyday personal finances.
- Retail: Our customers contribute to sustainable development.

These examples focus on the challenges—turned into opportunities—that these companies' customers or their customers' customers face. The alternative is to brainstorm new features for existing products and services. These are fundamentally different approaches. The former opens up opportunities for transformative leaps, in the right direction of the company's long-term goal, while the latter tends to prioritize the urgent over the important—the reactive over the proactive.

Principle 3: Influence Execution Substantially

It's not uncommon for organizations to meticulously craft strategic plans only to see them gather dust. It's like carefully configuring a gadget and never using it. This phenomenon, often called "set-and-forget," is a common pitfall.

While not dictating the specific "what" or "how," guiding star OKRs offer a structured process for integrating them into your daily decision-making. The planning, calibration, and cross-pollination make sure that your everyday actions align with your long-term goals and transform your strategy into an active force that influences execution, rather than a sidelined document.

Remember, every planned task is not derived from your guiding stars. Urgent matters, like fixing bugs, routine tasks, or addressing immediate problems, don't require a strategic direction—you simply act. Guiding stars are most effective in influencing transformative initiatives.

The "set-and-forget" approach, regrettably, is a common pitfall. It's akin to the plight of Sisyphus in Greek mythology, endlessly pushing a boulder uphill, only to watch it roll back down each time. Similarly, a strategic plan without consistent attention and adaptation becomes a Sisyphean struggle—a cycle of effort that ultimately yields little progress.

Principle 4: Use and Enhance Collective Intelligence

By interacting frequently and in many different ways, like the neurons in the brain, you create an overall intelligence greater than the sum of its parts. The collective intelligence that emerges through all this interaction is thus more than the accumulated knowledge that the individuals of the company possess.

Guiding stars aren't designed and controlled by a small group at the top. Instead, the entire organization observes, orients, decides, and acts in rapid and frequent loops. These loops are built into catchball, calibration, cross-pollination, and other guiding star practices and will happen automatically as a result.

Harnessing collective intelligence creates a self-reinforcing cycle of positive outcomes, including:

- *Innovative thinking:* The organization is more likely to uncover novel and creative solutions to complex problems when you bring together diverse expertise.

- *Faster adaptation:* The continuous flow of information from diverse sources enables the organization to respond more rapidly to changing market conditions and emerging opportunities.

- *Well-founded decisions:* By drawing on the collective wisdom of the entire organization, decisions are more likely to be sound, comprehensive, and aligned.

- *Sustainable solutions:* Inclusive decision-making processes tend to produce solutions that are more coherent and adaptable to long-term challenges.

- *Knowledge diffusion:* Everyone's understanding of the company's current state and strategic direction is enhanced when a wider range of perspectives are shared throughout the organization.

- *Increased engagement:* Employees feel more connected to the guiding stars when their input is valued, leading to higher levels of motivation and commitment.

Principle 5: Self-Organize for Scalability

In the realm of large organizations, micromanagement is counterproductive. When one person attempts to control every detail, it creates a bottleneck that impedes both quality and speed of delivery. Micromanagement doesn't scale.

In the workplace, individuals constantly interact and learn from their environment and colleagues. This constant exchange of ideas and information means it's impossible for any one person to have a complete understanding of everything that's going on. It's like trying to listen to every conversation in a crowded room.

That's why self-organization isn't simply an option—it's a natural consequence of people working together in a complex setting. Employees will always look for the best ways to work together and solve problems that come up. The graph on page 100 visually represents how employees (the dots) interact and collaborate (the lines), forming connections that may not perfectly align with the formal organizational chart (which, of course, still serves its own essential function). People want to get things done, and they'll instinctively reach out to the coworkers who can best help them.

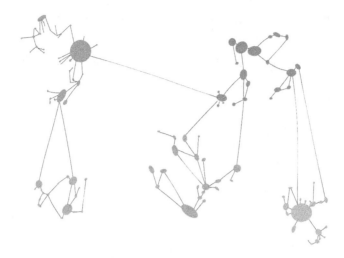

Imagine your brain guiding you towards learning a new skill—like playing tennis—without dictating the exact method. You experiment, try different approaches, and eventually find what works best for you. Similarly, with guiding star OKRs, the organization sets a shared direction, but it's up to the teams to self-organize and determine the most effective ways to reach that destination.

Successful self-organization is built by two-way relationships. When individuals influence and are influenced by their colleagues, a higher level of learning emerges. Self-organization forms the basis for principle 4, which states that you should use and enhance collective intelligence.

It's important to note that self-organization doesn't necessarily mean that the company will consist of entirely autonomous teams. There will always be dependencies between products, functions, and system components. Collaboration across silos, still decentralized, is beneficial to self-organizing teams.

Principle 6: Adapt Direction

Your strategic direction should be seamless, dynamic, and authentic. It's an ongoing process, not a one-time project. Similarly to how your brain constantly learns and adapts, new insights or changes in the environment can lead you to calibrate your guiding stars and the actions they cause, as shown in the image on page 101.

An adaptable strategic direction means having a clear vision that all employees understand and relate to while remaining flexible and open to adjustments based on feedback both from the market and employees. This is why a

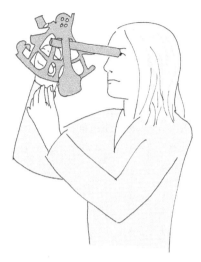

direction, rather than a goal, serves as a better decision-making tool for questions you don't yet know you'll ask.

Embracing new feedback means that being right from the start isn't the goal. That's why you over and over start from where you're at that point and look forward. This also entails that adjustments sometimes make incentive-based programs unfair. It's crucial to prioritize collective actions that benefit the company over an individual manager's pursuit of an outdated goal. Performance management isn't compatible with adaptive strategic execution.

Calibration is an example of how guiding star OKRs have adaptability built into the process. Important adjustments to the original plan happen automatically as you gain new insights.

Principle 7: Persist Through Timeboxing

Principle 6 (adapt) is balanced by principle 7 (persist) to avoid excessive volatility. While adaptability is essential, it doesn't mean constantly changing course. Persistence is key to seeing strategic execution through to completion. The teams should experience a stable environment while still being responsive to necessary adjustments.

You might know the Pomodoro Technique,[1] a time-management method that helps people focus. It's easy to lose momentum when colleagues talk and smartphones demand attention.

---

1. https://www.pragprog.com/titles/snfocus/pomodoro-technique-illustrated

In the Pomodoro Technique, you choose one single task, wind up a kitchen timer for 25 minutes, and trust your prioritization. New ideas? Keep working with the initial task. Phone rings? Keep working. Fire alarm? Keep working… well, there are limits. The point is to try to avoid even being tempted to switch tasks. You might not have finished your task when the timer rings. But you only promised to invest 25 minutes in this task, regardless of any sudden urge to switch. When the timer rings, after a short break you're finally allowed to reevaluate: continue with the same task or switch to a new one.

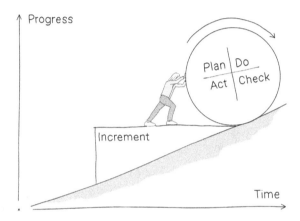

Timeboxing also works for strategic work in large groups of colleagues. You decide in advance how long to stick to a guiding star. When that time passes, you adjust as needed. Otherwise, you continue for another timebox. You might recognize this from lean and the iterative design and management method, Plan–Do–Check–Act (PDCA).

It's important to note that your horizon—the time frame being considered—can extend beyond the scope of your timebox. Your guiding star might describe something that could take several years to achieve (the horizon), and you decide to start by investing six months working towards this guiding star (the timebox). After six months, you make a new decision whether to continue working towards the same guiding star or switch to another. Both the frequency of planning and the time frame being considered typically expand as you move up the organizational hierarchy.

Applying the Principles to Guiding Star OKRs

Each of the seven principles presented in this chapter plays a crucial role in a successful implementation of the Guiding Star OKR framework. By incorporating these principles, guiding star OKRs create a more impactful, adaptable, and engaging approach to achieving the organizational strategic goals.

Here are three examples:

- Consider a scenario in which you develop a new product. Instead of focusing solely on meeting specific deadlines, you could prioritize giving customers new capabilities that address their unmet and unarticulated needs. This shift in focus encourages a more customer-centric approach, fostering innovation and differentiation in the market. See Chapter 3, Discovering Customer Opportunities, on page 29.

- To facilitate this process, you could encourage self-organization within the organization and create opportunities for random encounters and diverse perspectives. This could involve setting up cross-functional workshops, brainstorming sessions, and informal gatherings where employees from different departments can share their insights and ideas. See Chapter 7, Cross-Pollination: Everyone's Ears, Insights, and Ideas, on page 79.

- Instead of celebrating adherence to a predetermined plan, you could foster a culture of continuous adaptation. This would involve regularly reviewing and adjusting the strategic direction based on feedback from the market and the employees. See Chapter 6, Calibration: Fine-Tuning Guiding Stars, on page 65.

Of course, many other examples exist. As you can see, by integrating all seven principles, you create a dynamic and responsive organization that's well-equipped to navigate the complexities of modern business.

Key Takeaways

- In a dynamic world, setting a clear direction is more valuable than fixating on specific goals. This directional approach allows for flexibility and adaptation as circumstances change.

- Rather than focusing on incremental improvements, strategies solve significant challenges and create behavioral change for your customers or your customers' customers.

- A strategy isn't a static document but an active force that guides daily decision-making and actions throughout the organization.

- Engaging a diverse range of employees in the strategy process leads to better insights, more innovative solutions, and increased organizational alignment.

- Empowering teams to self-organize within a shared strategic direction fosters adaptability, innovation, and intrinsic motivation.

- The ability to adapt and refine strategies in response to new information and changing circumstances is crucial for long-term success.

- While it's important to maintain a consistent direction, being open to adjustments based on feedback and learning is equally important for navigating complex environments.

What's Next?

Even the best process can fail if not implemented well. The industry has seen disastrous results from attempts to introduce everything at once—the big bang. There are ways to let a process evolve step by step and, moreover, coevolve with the organization's own development. That's the theme for the next chapter.

CHAPTER 9

Implementing the Guiding Star OKR Framework

The moment has arrived to implement the Guiding Star OKR framework. The successful integration of the framework into your organization is critical to ensuring that your strategic endeavors are persistent, aligned, and adaptive.

While a comprehensive guide to change management and large-scale transformation is beyond the scope of this book, this chapter provides guiding principles for navigating the implementation process. We'll delve into how you can transform your organization by implementing one practice at a time in month-sized iterations while adapting to new insights that emerge during the transformation itself—that is, evolving toward change.

Preparing the Evolutionary Transformation

Before the organization can adopt the Guiding Star OKR framework, four preparatory steps are necessary. The first step is to understand the underlying purpose for implementing this framework at this particular time.

Step 1: Articulate Your Transformation "Why"

The introduction of guiding stars will inevitably impact many, if not all, of your colleagues. That's why it's essential to have a clear and compelling answer to the question, "Why are we doing this?" While this doesn't require a polished elevator pitch, a flawless vision of the future, or a quantifiable target, it's usually sufficient initially to simply identify the challenges that have prompted this initiative—that is, the challenges you're trying to overcome.

To ensure clarity and focus in your "whys," a helpful way to formulate them is to describe the problem you're trying to overcome in two sentences, preceded by one sentence describing the valuable outcome you want to achieve:

```
[valuable outcome]
    [your current problem]
```

The Guiding Star OKR framework can be beneficial in several scenarios. Take a moment to reflect on the following list, and consider which of these "whys"—perhaps even multiple—resonates with your organization's current reality.

Encourage proactive participation.

The development team is often overwhelmed with urgent tasks and struggles to find time for strategically important initiatives. They sometimes feel lost and lack a clear connection between their daily work and the company's overarching goals.

Achieve goals with OKRs.

The organization has previous experience with OKRs but has struggled to create engagement and achieve the desired results. Our goals were sometimes unclear or unrealistic, and there was a lack of a clear connection between the OKRs and our daily work.

Increase focus.

The organization lacks a clear, shared strategy, and there's a risk that different departments and teams are working in different directions. The management recognizes this and the team wants to create a more cohesive and goal-oriented organization.

Meet customers' real needs.

The company has a good understanding of its customers but wants to become even better at identifying and meeting customers' unspoken needs and desires. We want to create products that not only solve existing problems but also offer new possibilities and innovations.

Collaborate across silos.

The organization is divided into silos, and there are obstacles to collaboration and communication between different teams and departments. This leads to inefficiencies, duplication of work, and missed deadlines.

Innovate in a changing world.

The company tends to get stuck in old ruts and finds it difficult to adapt to market changes or technological developments. We want to become more agile and responsive to new trends and needs.

Strengthen employee motivation.
> Employees feel that they have limited control over their tasks and goals, leading to decreased motivation and engagement. We want to create a culture where all employees are more involved and responsible.

Now, consider whether any additional challenges are driving your initiative. Add them to your transformation "why" list, using the same syntax: two sentences describing the problem preceded by one sentence describing the valuable outcome you want to achieve.

The ideal number of transformation "whys" depends on the organization's current state. Too few "whys" may lead to overly radical and narrowly focused changes, and too many can dilute the message and create confusion. A rule of thumb is to have two to four "whys."

The list that you have created works well at the beginning of any articles, presentations, or other introductory materials you develop, even before you communicate about guiding stars in general. You'll need such material, especially for the overview that kicks off the evolutionary process. It also helps your transformation lead to stay on course.

Step 2: Nominate Your Transformation Lead

In the second preparatory step, you'll designate the individual or team who will spearhead and champion your transformation journey. The transformation lead acts as a catalyst for change, ensuring the process remains focused and aligned with your defined "whys."

Sometimes, it can be beneficial to share this role between an internal employee deeply familiar with the company culture and an external consultant who brings valuable perspectives and experiences from other organizations. This can create a powerful blend of insider knowledge and outside expertise. Alternatively, a single individual, whether internal or external, can effectively fulfill this role.

It's crucial not to reverse the order of steps 1 and 2. Articulating your "whys" first establishes a solid foundation for the transformation lead to build upon. It ensures the transformation is rooted in a broad understanding of the organization's needs and aspirations, rather than being driven by a single individual's agenda.

The transformation lead is a facilitative role, rather than being personally accountable for the outcome. The success of the transformation is a collective responsibility shared by the entire organization. The lead's role is to enable and support this collective effort.

In practical terms, this means the transformation lead will:

- Facilitate regular events and presentations to keep everyone informed and engaged in the transformation.

- Ensure the transformation roadmap is up-to-date and reflects progress and any shifts in direction.

- Serve as a central point of contact for questions and concerns related to the transformation.

Step 3: Visualize the Transformation Roadmap

Rather than defining a fixed plan upfront, in step 3 your transformation lead creates a roadmap inspired by Now-Next-Later[1] to provide a shared—that is, centrally located and accessible to all—visualization of your journey. It clearly shows what's underway, while leaving room for flexibility and adaptation. Divide ongoing and potentially upcoming initiatives into three classes:

- *Now:* What has been started and not finished
- *Next:* Candidates for the next iteration
- *Later:* What's interesting but not currently a candidate

The roadmap may evolve in unexpected ways, and that's perfectly normal. There will be times when things don't unfold as you originally envisioned. Embrace these moments as opportunities for growth and adaptation. Your ability to navigate unforeseen challenges and adjust course is a fundamental aspect of the organization's evolutionary change process.

---

1.   https://www.prodpad.com/blog/invented-now-next-later-roadmap

The transformation lead actively manages the roadmap throughout the entire transformation, typically updating it at the conclusion of each evolutionary iteration.

Step 4: Introduce the Guiding Stars Transformation Broadly

The fourth step in preparing for the actual evolutionary transformation is relatively straightforward. The transformation lead ensures that everyone directly or indirectly impacted by the transformation receives the same one-hour overview of the Guiding Star OKR framework.

You'll begin by revisiting the purpose—the "whys"—that you defined in step 1 and illustrate how the framework can empower the company to reach its goals. It's crucial to emphasize that this is an evolving process. You're not seeking the perfect solution right away—instead, it's about continuous learning and improvement.

Additionally, the transformation lead will share the first draft of the evolutionary transformation roadmap. Make sure that everyone understands that this isn't a rigid project plan, but rather a more authentic way for the organization to understand what lies ahead. It's a flexible guide that will adapt as we learn and grow together throughout this journey.

After this fourth step, it's time to set the transformation in motion.

Iterate the Transformation

The evolutionary approach to adopting the Guiding Star OKR framework involves taking small but consistent steps. One step, also known as "iteration," lasts for one month. Introduce no more or less than one new practice in each iteration. Since circumstances vary between companies, each company knows best which practice to start with—added in the "now" section—and how to divide the other potential practices between "next" and "later."

The following is an unordered list of potential practices that can be implemented within a single iteration:

- The catchball process
- The sponsor and liaison roles for all guiding stars
- Calibration sessions
- Cross-pollination sessions
- Pupation
- O&O from the discovery process

If the monthly pace of change feels too daunting, reduce the scope of each iteration rather than slow down the overall frequency of change. For example, implement the catchball process on one level per iteration rather than all at once. The goal is to maintain a sense of continuous progress without overwhelming the organization's members.

The objective of an iteration is to become familiar with the new working methods, not to achieve perfection. What you introduce in one iteration will naturally improve in subsequent iterations as you gain more experience with what works well.

Ambassadors: Your Allies in the Change Effort

By now, you may be wondering how to get the entire organization on board with this journey to a new framework. That's where ambassadors come in. They are passionate individuals who want to promote the change and support their colleagues.

Being an ambassador is voluntary, but it means taking on extra responsibility to ensure that the framework becomes a natural part of everyday life. Capture the interest of potential ambassadors during the introductory presentation and continuously during the iteration events.

The ambassadors aren't only your eyes and ears in the organization—they are also your extended arm. By giving them knowledge and trust, they become invaluable in the work of creating a successful adoption of the framework.

The Iteration Schedule

No two iterations are exactly alike, especially as you introduce a unique practice in each one. But there's naturally a recurring backbone—a schedule—for the iterations.

1. *Introduce this month's new practice.*

    Kick off each month with a lean coffee[2] session where you present the new practice you're about to introduce in this iteration. The invitation to this session is open to everyone to foster transparency, but participation is up to each individual. This session also serves as an excellent opportunity to identify and recruit new ambassadors.

2. *Define guiding principles.*

    Following the initial lean coffee session, the transformation lead extracts guiding principles for how you'll work. The principles are based on the discussions during the session and the lead's own experience. Formatted as "Prioritize X over Y," the principles should reflect this adaptive mindset and encourage experimentation and flexibility.

    The principles apply only to the practice that's new this month. For example, if you're introducing catchball, a principle could be: "Prioritize open dialogue and feedback over strict compliance with a predefined plan." For introducing cross-pollination, a principle might be: "Prioritize spontaneous idea generation and knowledge sharing over structured agendas and presentations." Choose between one and four principles that are specific to your company. Another company would choose different principles because they have a different culture, size, maturity, and other factors.

    The transformation lead shares the principles with everyone involved. But don't wait for that to be finalized before starting the experiment itself.

3. *Try the new practice.*

    Follow up the lean coffee session by frequently visiting different parts of the organization to see how the introduction of the new practice is going and to spread enthusiasm.

    The ambassadors give you leverage if the organization supports them thoughtfully. Create a safe space for them to meet now and then and share experiences through regular lean coffee sessions. Here, they can talk about both their successes and challenges and work together to find solutions.

---

2. https://leancoffee.org

4. *Share insights.*

Finally, end the month with an open space technology (see *Open Space Technology: A User's Guide [Owe97]*) session where everyone can share their insights and lessons learned.

Remember, this is a shared journey. By involving everyone in the process, creating space for experimentation and learning, and providing feedback along the way, you can create change that is both embedded and adaptive. As with the iteration's initial lean coffee, this session is an opportunity to identify and recruit new ambassadors.

5. *Update the roadmap.*

After the open space session, the transformation lead updates the Now-Next-Later transformation roadmap. Sometimes the lead adds entirely new practices on the board, while others might disappear. What always happens is that the lead replaces the content in the "now" category with the next month's new practice. Often, but not always, one or more things also move from "later" to "next."

Why Not Linear Implementation?

Understandably, some in the organization may express impatience, suggesting that adopting guiding stars should be as simple as replicating a competitor's approach. But it's important to recognize that each organization has a unique history, culture, and workforce. The following considerations can help illustrate why a linear, one-size-fits-all approach to change may not be effective in this particular context.

Evolutionary processes, with their ability to incrementally build on previous successes and explore countless possibilities, are perfect for creating complex systems, such as the human eye—a structure so intricate that it would be nearly impossible to design from scratch. On the other hand, when faced with well-defined problems with predictable parameters, such as optimizing a supply chain, linear processes, and advanced algorithms can excel by methodically analyzing data and finding the most efficient solution, as shown in the image on page 113.

There's a plethora of popular linear change models. Primarily, they present change as a sequential process with clear steps or phases to be followed in a specific order. The change plan is detailed, and deviations are often classified as problems.

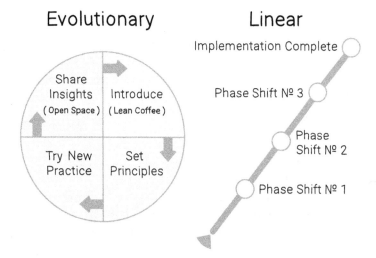

While linear change models can be useful for structuring and understanding change processes, they can also be limiting in situations where change is more complex, uncertain, or requires a more flexible and adaptive strategy. The process of introducing innovative collaborative methods for product and service development in a large organization, particularly one with a highly skilled workforce, is an excellent example of complex change. Evolutionary change differs from traditional linear models in many ways:

Complexity and adaptability

Evolutionary change acknowledges that organizations and their environments are complex and constantly changing. Rather than trying to control and predict every step, it focuses on building adaptability and the ability to respond to unforeseen events.

Experimentation and learning

Rather than following a predetermined plan, evolutionary change encourages experimentation and learning. By testing new ideas and methods in rapid iterations, the organization can reduce risk while learning what works and what doesn't and then adapt accordingly.

Decentralized decision-making and self-organization

Instead of relying on a central management group to make all decisions, evolutionary change allows for decentralized decision-making and self-organization. This allows teams and individuals closest to the problem to make decisions and act quickly.

Diversity and inclusion

By incorporating diverse perspectives and ideas, the organization can become more innovative and adaptable. But true inclusion goes beyond simply assembling a diverse group. While an evolutionary approach promotes collaboration and openness, fostering inclusion also requires actively breaking down barriers and ensuring everyone feels welcome and valued. As Verna Myers eloquently states, "Diversity is being invited to the party; inclusion is being asked to dance."[3]

Continuous feedback and improvement

Rather than viewing change as a one-time project, evolutionary change views it as a continuous process of feedback and improvement. By constantly gathering and analyzing data, the organization can identify areas for improvement and make adjustments in real time.

As you read this list, you may think that the process of establishing the Guiding Star OKR framework is similar to the journey of pursuing your guiding stars once the framework is in place. While some similarities exist, it's important to recognize the key distinctions between these two phases.

More than Just Following the Stars

It's important to understand the significant differences between adopting the Guiding Star OKR framework and pursuing your guiding stars once the framework is in place.

- *Focus*: Guiding stars are about creating value for your customers and their customers. Adopting the framework, on the other hand, is about improving the effectiveness in your organization.

- *Scope*: Guiding stars primarily affect the teams that work directly on related tasks. Your implementation of the framework can affect everyone in your organization, directly or indirectly. In addition to these differences, you should consider other important aspects:

- *Time horizon*: Guiding stars are your long-term and ambitious goals. A single iteration of your implementation of the framework has a clearer timeline.

- *Measurement*: Guiding stars are quantified by key results that directly reflect your customer's impact. Your implementation of the framework

---

3.   https://www.youtube.com/watch?v=9gS2VPUkB3M

can be evaluated through other metrics, such as employee engagement or improvements in your internal processes.

- *Change management*: Adopting the Guiding Star OKR framework requires a significant shift in mindset and culture throughout the organization. Pursuing your guiding stars also requires change, but perhaps not a fundamental transformation.

- *Leadership and support*: Adopting the framework requires strong leadership and support from top management. Your guiding stars also benefit from leadership support, but their success may depend more on the collective effort and ownership of different teams and individuals.

In addition to the practical differences, there's also an important emotional aspect to consider.

- *Motivation and engagement*: Changing one's working methods and routines can be challenging and requires significant effort. It can sometimes feel abstract and difficult to see the direct benefits. On the other hand, the work of developing products or services that change the way other companies operate can be more inspiring and motivating. Seeing the positive impact you have on others can create a sense of meaning and purpose.

You should be aware of this potential difference in motivation and actively work to create engagement and excitement around the implementation of the Guiding Star OKR framework. By clearly communicating the purpose and benefits of the framework and involving colleagues in the process, you can increase motivation and ensure that everyone feels a part of the change. Ambassadors can amplify this motivation.

Key Takeaways

- Clearly define the reasons for adopting the Guiding Star OKR framework, ensuring that everyone understands the challenges you're trying to overcome and the value it brings.

- Take an iterative approach, introducing changes gradually to avoid overwhelming the organization and to allow for adaptation and learning.

- Use a visual roadmap to communicate the transformation journey, showing current progress and potential future steps while maintaining flexibility.

- Acknowledge that the implementation path may evolve, and view unforeseen challenges as opportunities for growth and learning.

- Foster a sense of collective ownership by involving everyone in the process, encouraging open communication, and valuing diverse perspectives.

- Recognize the potential difference in motivation between adopting the framework and pursuing guiding stars, and actively work to create engagement and enthusiasm throughout the process.

- Identify and support passionate individuals who can act as ambassadors, and provide them with resources and opportunities to share their knowledge and enthusiasm.

What's Next?

Implementing the Guiding Star OKR framework can be challenging. It's easy to overlook important details and fall into common traps. The next chapter identifies these challenges and offers suggestions for addressing them.

CHAPTER 10

Overcoming Guiding Star Challenges

In the course of guiding teams through their Guiding Star OKR implementations, I've discovered many challenges occur around four main areas: implementation and adoption, leadership, culture, and strategy and goals. In this chapter, I'll share insights into these common hurdles and offer practical solutions to help you navigate them successfully.

For each area, we'll delve into five of the most common questions I've received from teams embarking on this journey to provide you with the knowledge and tools to overcome obstacles and foster a thriving OKR culture within the organization. Sometimes, all it takes is a shift in perspective—a new way of talking about things—to make something that seemed complicated suddenly feel natural.

Implementation and Adoption

Embarking on a new framework like Guiding Star OKRs can naturally raise questions about its practical implementation. You may wonder how to integrate it seamlessly into your existing workflow without causing disruption or adding unnecessary burdens. Rest assured, the framework is adaptable and can be tailored to your organization's unique rhythm and structure. It's all about enhancing your current practices, not replacing them entirely. The journey to effective strategy execution is an evolving process, as shown in the image on page 118.

The Guiding Star OKR framework seems to require a significant time commitment. How can we implement it without overwhelming employees and impacting productivity?

Concerns about increased workload are valid. The key is to implement the framework gradually, one practice at a time. This allows your team to adapt and learn without feeling overwhelmed. As you introduce new

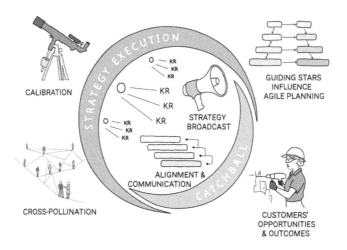

elements, such as catchball or calibration, encourage employees to identify existing processes that may become redundant. For instance, lengthy status update meetings could be replaced with more dynamic cross-pollination sessions.

The goal is to evolve your existing ways of working, not add more to the pile. By actively involving employees in this process, you'll foster a sense of ownership and ensure that the framework integrates seamlessly into your workflow.

The book mentions the importance of adapting the implementation process to the specific context of the organization. How do we tailor the framework to our unique culture and challenges?

The good news is that you don't need to have all the answers up front. Instead of trying to predict the perfect fit, start by introducing a practice that seems both achievable and valuable in your current context.

Every company has its own unique culture, but your culture is also constantly evolving. As you implement a new practice, allow it to interact with your existing ways of working. Think of it as an experiment in which both the framework and your culture will shape each other in unpredictable ways. Making small changes at a time means lower risk.

By actively involving your team in this process, you'll gain valuable insights and ensure that the framework organically adapts to your specific needs. Embrace the journey of discovery, and you'll find that the Guiding Star OKR framework becomes a natural extension of your ever-evolving and unique organizational identity.

The concept of a transformation lead is important, but how do we ensure that our transformation leads have the support and resources necessary to guide the organization through the change process?

The responsibility for change doesn't rest solely with the transformation lead. It's a collective effort that requires buy-in and commitment from the entire organization. By fostering a culture of transparency and open communication, you empower every team member to contribute to the process.

Start by implementing the framework gradually in iterations. This will allow you to adjust resource allocation as needed and ensure that the transformation lead has the support they need without overcommitting up front. By involving everyone in the journey, you create a sense of shared ownership and increase the likelihood of success.

By investing in the development of ambassadors through time, resources, and training, you enable them to become valuable partners to the transformation lead, driving local adoption and commitment.

How can we successfully implement this framework at scale, ensuring it works seamlessly across our entire organization?

The Guiding Star OKR framework isn't a one-size-fits-all solution. Factors such as your organization's size and complexity will influence how you implement and adapt the framework. If your organization has multiple levels, consider a phased approach that introduces the framework one level at a time. This helps avoid the challenges of managing too many changes in different contexts at the same time. Also, avoid small pilot projects in isolated parts of the organization, as their success may not be transferable to other areas with different dynamics.

Be prepared to adapt your implementation as you gain new insights, but don't try to design all the adaptations in advance. By embracing flexibility and learning from experience, you can ensure that the Guiding Star OKR framework remains a valuable tool as your organization evolves.

We prefer a different approach to planning than timeboxed quarters and sprints (as in agile). Would the Guiding Star OKR framework still be a good fit for our planning needs?

Absolutely. The Guiding Star OKR framework can be valuable, even if your organization doesn't use timebox planning. The core principles of the framework are adaptable to different planning and execution approaches. The essence of the framework is to promote a shared strategic direction, foster collaboration, and enable adaptability. These principles are beneficial, regardless of your specific planning methodology. You can still use catchball for collaborative goal setting, calibration for ongoing adjustments, and cross-pollination for knowledge sharing and innovation.

The key is to integrate the framework's principles into your existing processes. For example, instead of pupation sessions tied to timeboxed iterations, you could have regular strategy reviews aligned with your planning cycles. The focus remains on maintaining a clear strategic direction, fostering collaboration, and adapting to change, regardless of your specific planning approach.

Leadership

The shift to a more decentralized and adaptive approach to leadership can be both exciting and challenging. You might have concerns about maintaining accountability and ensuring that teams remain aligned with the overarching strategic vision. The Guiding Star OKR framework empowers leaders to foster a culture of trust, transparency, and shared responsibility. It's about guiding the ship, not controlling every oar stroke.

The book mentions the importance of avoiding micromanagement. How can we provide guidance and support without stifling self-organization and creativity?
It's a delicate balance to avoid micromanagement while still providing guidance and support—especially when transitioning to a framework that emphasizes self-organization and empowerment. In addition to stifling creativity, micromanagement hinders performance by creating bottlenecks and limiting growth opportunities. Instead of dictating every step, focus on creating an environment where employees can thrive.

Foster a motivating environment by building strong relationships, encouraging participation in decision-making, and taking the long-term view. At the same time, cultivate a learning environment in which employees are empowered to discover solutions, leaders demonstrate enthusiasm and engagement, and support is readily available when needed. By shifting your focus from controlling tasks to nurturing growth, you'll empower your team to reach their full potential while maintaining a supportive and collaborative atmosphere.

The book advocates a decentralized decision-making process. How can we uphold accountability and avoid decision paralysis?

The shift toward distributed decision-making can feel unfamiliar. The Guiding Star OKR framework provides mechanisms to ensure accountability and prevent decision paralysis.

Centralizing decision-making often creates bottlenecks, bureaucracy, and a lack of ownership. In a complex organization with numerous daily interactions, no one person can have all the information necessary to make every decision. Imposing centralized control only adds another layer of complexity.

Instead of trying to anticipate every possible scenario and make decisions in advance, leaders should focus on creating a culture of transparency and frequent feedback loops. By actively participating in demos, reviews, and other knowledge-sharing opportunities, leaders gain valuable insights into the reality of the work being done. This enables them to make informed strategic decisions without micromanaging day-to-day activities. Remember, the goal is to empower teams to make decisions closest to their work while maintaining alignment with the overall strategic direction.

The concept of a guiding star liaison is interesting, but how can we confirm the liaison possesses the required skills and authority to facilitate collaboration and knowledge sharing effectively?

Ensuring guiding star liaisons have the necessary skills and authority is essential for their success. A combination of training, experience, and domain expertise is key. Prioritize training potential liaisons in agile leadership and meeting facilitation. Initially, pair new liaisons with experienced ones, and establish a mentorship program for ongoing support.

Select liaisons who already possess relevant domain knowledge and who understand the context of the guiding star—for example, a team coach from one of the contributing teams. Provide them with a well-developed and up-to-date O&O artifact to guide their work. This will empower them to focus on facilitation rather than building the foundation from scratch.

Finally, recognize and reward the liaison role as a valuable career path within your organization. By investing in their development and acknowledging their contributions, you'll foster a pool of skilled liaisons ready to drive collaboration and knowledge sharing across teams.

The concept of self-organization seems appealing, but how do we maintain control and ensure that teams are working in the overall strategic direction?

The Guiding Star OKR framework addresses this balance through a combination of practices that promote both self-organization and alignment. Catchball, for instance, allows teams to contribute to the overall strategic direction while maintaining the flexibility to set some of their own local guiding stars. Pupation sessions ensure that work toward long-term goals isn't completely overshadowed by urgent tasks. Calibration and cross-pollination sessions create a shared understanding and alignment across teams.

By actively involving teams, managers, and all other stakeholders in these practices, the framework encourages a sense of ownership and shared responsibility for achieving the organization's strategic goals. It's not about imposing control but about fostering a collaborative environment where teams are empowered to make decisions within a clear strategic context.

The book advocates adaptability and flexibility. How can we avoid constant changes in direction that can lead to confusion and instability?

While the Guiding Star OKR framework emphasizes adaptability, it's important to strike a balance between flexibility and maintaining a clear strategic focus. The key is to maintain the presence and relevance of your long-term goals. Cross-pollination sessions help keep employees focused on their guiding stars, while calibration sessions allow for fine-tuning and adjustments to ensure goals remain aligned with the current reality.

Clear communication is also essential. By formulating OKRs from the customers' perspective and providing a well-structured and accessible O&O artifact, you ensure everyone understands the strategic direction.

Finally, involving employees in shaping these long-term goals from the outset fosters a sense of ownership and motivation. Practices such as catchball, strategy broadcast, and pupation provide opportunities for active participation and ensure that everyone is invested in the journey.

Culture

Cultivating a culture of innovation and continuous learning requires a delicate balance. You may worry that embracing quenched disorder (see Chapter 7,

Cross-Pollination: Everyone's Ears, Insights, and Ideas, on page 79) could lead to chaos or emphasizing experimentation could compromise efficiency. The Guiding Star OKR framework provides a structured approach to fostering creativity and adaptability. It's about creating an environment where ideas can flow freely and risk is encouraged, all within a framework that maintains organizational focus and alignment with direction.

The book emphasizes the importance of continuous learning and improvement. How do we create a culture that embraces experimentation and views unexpected outcomes as opportunities for growth?

The goal of quenched disorder is to create a bounded environment in which innovative ideas can emerge without sacrificing stability. Cross-pollination sessions, as described in the book, offer a safe and structured way to introduce quenched disorder. These timeboxed events encourage spontaneous interactions and the exploration of new ideas, all within a focused context related to your guiding stars. They provide a space for thought experimentation without disrupting your day-to-day operations.

In addition, by strengthening and expanding your employees' informal networks, your cross-pollination sessions create opportunities for natural collaboration across silo borders and hierarchical levels in their daily work, increasing the likelihood of discovering disruptive ideas.

Innovation often arises from unexpected connections. Quenched disorder, facilitated through cross-pollination, creates the conditions for these connections to occur, enabling your organization to tap into its potential collective intelligence and discover groundbreaking solutions.

The Guiding Star OKR framework seems to require a high level of trust and transparency. How do we build and maintain trust in organizations with hierarchical structures or a history of top-down management?

Bridging the gap between transparency and hierarchy is key. The Guiding Star OKR framework offers a pathway to cultivate trust and collaboration, even in environments with a history of top-down management.

Trust can't be commanded or forced; it's earned through shared experiences and mutual respect. The Guiding Star OKR framework emphasizes collaboration through practices such as catchball, pupation, cross-pollination, and calibration. These events allow individuals to work together toward shared goals, organically building trust along the way.

Working collaboratively toward shared guiding stars breaks down informal silos and encourages interaction across levels, fostering a sense of collective responsibility and shared purpose. When people see their colleagues actively contributing and demonstrating competence, trust naturally grows.

If skepticism arises, transparency is a powerful antidote. Encourage leaders to actively participate in demos and reviews so that they can witness firsthand the progress being made and the challenges being overcome. Open communication and access to information will further build trust and dispel any doubts.

Building trust takes time and effort, but it's an investment that pays off in improved collaboration, innovation, and overall organizational performance. By embracing the collaborative spirit of the Guiding Star OKR framework, even hierarchical organizations can cultivate a culture of trust and achieve remarkable results.

While the book offers valuable insights into strategy execution, its detailed approach and scientific analogies might not resonate with busy executives. Would using business-oriented language in an executive summary make the framework more appealing and accessible to them?

While it's natural to consider adapting the language for a busy C-level executive, it's important to understand that traditional business terms, often rooted in Industrial Age machine metaphors, may not always effectively capture the essence of large-scale collaboration. Machine metaphors work well for describing routines and predictable tasks, but they fail to capture the emergent collaboration and adaptability required in today's complex business world. In my experience, senior leaders often find scientific analogies more relatable and insightful when it comes to understanding the dynamics of large-scale collaboration and strategic execution.

Simply translating the framework into traditional business terms risks oversimplifying its concepts and perpetuating the illusion that outcomes are always predictable and controllable. Instead, consider harnessing the power of scientific metaphors to spark curiosity and convey the framework's focus on adaptability, learning, and collective intelligence. This approach may resonate more deeply with top management seeking innovative solutions for navigating complexity.

What can we do when low participation in voluntary meetings, such as cross-pollination, becomes a challenge?

Low participation in voluntary meetings, such as cross-pollination, is a common challenge, especially when employees are already juggling busy schedules. Understandably, they may be reluctant to commit to additional meetings if they don't see a clear benefit or relevance to their work.

One success factor is to ensure that these voluntary meetings are well-prepared and structured to maximize value. Clearly communicate the purpose and desired outcomes of each meeting, highlighting how participation can help achieve the guiding stars. Consider offering a variety of topics or formats to accommodate different interests and learning styles.

In addition, explore ways to incorporate cross-pollination into existing workflows. For example, you could devote a portion of regular team meetings to cross-pollination activities or encourage informal knowledge-sharing sessions within teams.

Finally, recognize and celebrate the contributions of those who participate in voluntary meetings. This can create a positive feedback loop encouraging others to join in and experience the benefits of cross-pollination firsthand.

We're concerned that management is trying to burden us with more work and doesn't trust us to do our jobs effectively. How can we find the time to implement the Guiding Star OKR framework without sacrificing our core responsibilities?

Initial hesitation toward new processes is natural, especially if it seems like it might create additional work. But the Guiding Star OKR framework is designed to enhance efficiency and focus, ultimately freeing up time for your core responsibilities. Instead of only adding more meetings, the framework encourages you to identify existing meetings or processes that may be redundant or less effective. As you implement the Guiding Star OKRs, you'll likely discover opportunities to streamline communication and eliminate unnecessary bureaucracy, freeing up valuable time for meaningful work.

In addition, the framework's emphasis on prioritizing the important over the urgent helps teams reduce multitasking and focus on activities that truly drive progress toward strategic goals. By aligning everyone's efforts and fostering a culture of collaboration, the Guiding Star OKR framework results in increased efficiency and productivity, allowing you to achieve more with less.

Strategy and Goals

Navigating the complexities of strategy execution in a large organization can be daunting. You may have questions about managing dependencies between teams, measuring long-term impact, or balancing short-term needs with long-term aspirations. The Guiding Star OKR framework provides a holistic approach to strategy and goal setting that fosters collaboration and adaptability. It's about creating a shared vision that empowers teams to make informed decisions and take ownership of their contributions.

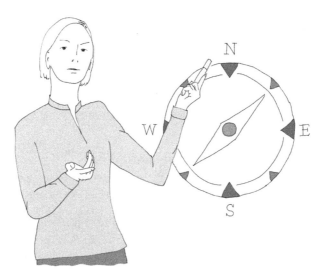

The team of teams concept seems ideal, but how do we manage dependencies and ensure coordination between different teams working toward the same guiding star?

In general, a decentralized approach can, at worst, lead to fragmentation and misalignment. The Guiding Star OKR framework is designed to address this challenge—particularly in complex organizations with multiple dependencies. Rather than focusing solely on individual team deliverables, the framework prioritizes overall strategic direction—long term over near term. This shared focus encourages your teams to collaborate and communicate proactively, ensuring that their efforts contribute to the bigger picture.

Cross-pollination sessions play a vital role in fostering this collaboration. By creating opportunities for open dialogue and knowledge sharing across teams, these sessions help you identify and address dependencies early on. They also promote a common understanding of your long-term goals and their implications, which is often difficult to achieve in traditional project review meetings.

Remember, the ultimate priority is to make progress toward your long-term goals, not only to complete individual tasks—creating value rather than simply being busy. The Guiding Star OKR framework empowers your teams to self-organize and collaborate effectively, ensuring that their dependencies are managed and that coordination is maintained in pursuit of the shared vision.

In large organizations, misaligned team objectives and inter-team dependencies can lead to conflicts and prioritization challenges. How can we achieve strategic alignment and effective collaboration without sacrificing team-level autonomy and engagement in large organizations?

Misaligned projects and inter-team dependencies are common challenges in large organizations, leading to a desire for a single, unifying objective. But enforcing a company-wide objective that lacks relevance to most teams' specific work, can lead to disengagement at their level. The Guiding Star OKR framework presents an alternative solution.

Guiding stars chart a long-term strategic direction without predetermined scope and activities. This allows for flexibility and adaptation as circumstances change, reducing the conflicts and prioritization issues that arise in traditional project management.

Remember, the primary goal is to achieve important long-term objectives, not to keep everyone on task all the time. It's perfectly acceptable if every team isn't directly involved in every guiding star. Shared goals are valuable, but individual teams can also make their own unique contributions. By prioritizing strategic alignment and fostering collaboration through practices such as cross-pollination and calibration, the Guiding Star OKR framework empowers your teams to self-organize to work toward a shared vision, ensuring that even a large and complex organization can move in a unified direction.

The Guiding Star OKR framework seems to require a significant shift in mindset and culture. How do we overcome resistance to change and ensure that employees at all levels embrace it?

People are generally open to change when they buy into the reasons for it and see how it can lead to improvement. Instead of simply imposing the framework, focus on transparent communication and active listening. Clearly articulate the "why" behind the transformation, highlighting the challenges you're addressing and the benefits you expect to achieve.

Encourage participation and feedback from employees at all levels. This not only helps identify and address concerns early on but also creates a sense of shared ownership of the change. The Guiding Star OKR framework is adaptable, and local adaptations aren't only expected but encouraged. By framing training and guidance as principles rather than rigid rules, you empower employees to take ownership of implementation and tailor it to their specific contexts. This fosters a sense of autonomy and encourages self-organization, ultimately leading to a more successful and sustainable transformation.

I don't see the need for cascading goal setting—breaking down goals and delegating subgoals. What if our managers want it?

The desire for cascading goal-setting is popular in environments accustomed to traditional top-down planning of well-known work items. But the Guiding Star OKR framework encourages a different approach. Unlike work items or tasks, goals and strategic directions cannot simply be broken down into subgoals. If there's a desire to do so, it may indicate that the focus has shifted prematurely to solutions and implementation details. That's fine, but it's important to recognize that this isn't part of your goal-setting process itself. You've moved on from "why" to "what."

By starting with the "why" (the goals) and then moving on to the "what" (the work items), we can ensure that strategy truly guides execution. If someone wants to break down the goals, take a step back and confirm first that everyone understands and agrees on the desired direction. Only then should you move on to planning the execution, focusing on the activities and solutions that will move you in that direction.

Lower-level goals can certainly contribute to higher-level ones, but it's not about creating a perfect puzzle in which all the pieces fit together neatly. Reality is more complex, and that's precisely why we set the direction together first and then explore solutions and tasks.

How can we establish the right number of guiding stars to avoid a lack of focus and diluted efforts?

Determining the ideal number of guiding stars can be challenging, and it's unlikely to be perfect every time. The Guiding Star OKR framework emphasizes flexibility and adaptation, so it's okay to experiment and adjust as you learn. One clear sign that you have too many guiding stars is when they start competing for the same resources—financial, human, or other—forcing you to prioritize one goal over another. Remember, work items can be prioritized, but strategic goals and directions shouldn't. If you find yourself in this situation, it's a strong indication that you need to reduce the number of guiding stars.

On the other hand, having too few guiding stars can lead to limited engagement, as only a small portion of the organization may be able to contribute directly. But it's important to remember that not everyone needs to be actively working on guiding star initiatives at all times. Some colleagues will naturally focus on business-as-usual activities rather than transformative leaps.

As a general guideline, aim for one to three concurrent guiding stars at any given level. It's often better to start with fewer and gradually increase the number as you gain experience and confidence in the framework. The goal is to find the right balance that fosters focus, engagement, and strategic alignment without overwhelming your team.

Key Takeaways

- Implementing the Guiding Star OKR framework is an ongoing process of learning and adaptation, not a one-time event.

- Adapt the framework to your organization's unique culture and challenges, fostering a sense of ownership and seamless integration.

- Provide the transformation lead with the necessary support, resources, and authority to guide the change effectively.

- Embrace adaptability while maintaining a clear strategic direction to avoid confusion and instability.

- Build trust through open communication, collaboration, and active participation from all levels of the organization.

- Ensure that goals are aligned across teams and departments, fostering collaboration and minimizing conflicts.

- Clearly articulate the reasons behind adopting the framework, emphasizing the challenges you're addressing and the benefits you aim to achieve.

What's Next?

It's time to take your Guiding Stars out into the world and see how they work in practice! I'd love to hear about your experiences—the good, the bad, and the unexpected. Share any insights you gain, or if you find something I might have overlooked. And hey, if you have any ideas on how to make the Guiding Star OKR framework even better, I'm all ears!

Who knows, maybe down the road we'll cross paths at a conference and can swap stories over coffee. We can even laugh about any missteps along the way. After all, who says it has to be perfect from day one? The important thing is that we keep learning and contribute to the community.

Best of luck with your Guiding Stars!

Glossary

Agile Planning: An iterative and incremental approach to planning and executing work, emphasizing flexibility, collaboration, and customer value.

Alignment: The state of agreement and coordination between different teams and individuals within an organization, working towards a shared purpose.

Ambassadors: Passionate individuals who voluntarily champion the adoption of the Guiding Star OKR framework, supporting their colleagues and promoting its benefits.

Annealed Disorder: A state of structured order and predictability, often associated with formal meetings and processes, which can be valuable but may limit innovation.

Autocatalysis: A self-reinforcing process where the outcome of an action or interaction further accelerates or amplifies that same action or interaction, leading to exponential growth or change.

Backlog: A prioritized list of work items that a development team plans to engage with in future sprints or iterations.

Big OODA: The application of the OODA loop at an organizational level, involving everyone in the process of observing, orienting, deciding, and acting to enhance agility and responsiveness.

Cadence: The rhythm or frequency at which goals are set and reviewed. Different levels of the organization may have different cadences based on their scope and responsibilities.

Calibration: Regular sessions where teams and individuals assess progress toward their guiding stars, make adjustments as needed, and ensure alignment with the overall strategy.

Cascading OKRs: A discouraged practice where objectives are broken down into smaller, isolated tasks and assigned to individual teams, potentially hindering collaboration and adaptability.

Catchball: A collaborative process where ideas and feedback are exchanged between different levels of the organization, ensuring everyone has a voice in shaping the strategic direction.

Coevolution: The process where two or more entities, such as businesses and their customers, mutually influence each other's development and adaptation over time.

Composite Key Results: Key results that combine multiple properties to provide a more comprehensive and nuanced understanding of progress toward an objective.

Context-Free Key Results: Key results that focus on a single metric or factor without considering the broader context or interdependencies within a system.

Cross-Pollination: Facilitated events that encourage spontaneous interactions and knowledge sharing across teams and departments, fostering innovation and collective intelligence.

Customer Opportunities: Areas where customers experience pain points, frustrations, or unmet needs, representing potential areas for innovation and improvement.

Customer Outcomes: The desired future state or positive impact that customers hope to achieve by using a product or service.

Customer Value Chain: The series of activities and processes that a company undertakes to create and deliver value to its customers.

Customer-Centric: An approach that prioritizes understanding and fulfilling customer needs and expectations throughout the product development and strategy execution process.

Emergent Collaboration: The spontaneous and self-organized cooperation that arises when individuals with diverse skills and perspectives come together to solve a problem or achieve a goal.

Epics: Large, complex work items that are broken down into smaller, more manageable features or user stories for development and planning purposes.

Execution: The process of putting the strategy into action. In the context of Guiding Star OKR framework, it's influenced by the strategic direction set by the guiding stars. See the sidebar, *What "Strategy" and "Execution" Mean in This Book.*

What "Strategy" and "Execution" Mean in This Book

In this book, strategy is presented as the overarching plan or direction to achieve a long-term goal or vision. It involves making conscious choices in a way that maximizes the chances of success.

Strategy isn't only about setting goals but also about understanding the surrounding environment and identifying your customers' opportunities and desired outcomes. This book emphasizes that a strategy benefits from being based on the organization's collective knowledge.

Execution is the process of putting the strategy into practice and moving in the agreed direction through concrete actions and decisions. It's about organizing, coordinating, and leading resources and people to achieve the set goals.

Determined execution is required for the strategy to be successful. This book emphasizes that execution requires persistence, alignment, and the ability to adapt to changes and new insights. Execution is also about creating a culture where everyone in the organization is engaged and working towards the same goals.

Extrinsic Motivation: The motivation to perform an activity to earn a reward or avoid punishment, often driven by external factors.

Guiding Star Liaison: A facilitator who fosters collaboration and knowledge exchange within the team of teams working towards a guiding star, ensuring smooth progress and adaptation.

Guiding Star OKRs: A goal-setting framework that combines the traditional OKR (objectives and key results) approach with a focus on long-term strategic direction, fostering adaptability and collaboration within organizations.

Guiding Star Sponsor: The individual or team responsible for proposing and championing a specific guiding star, ensuring clarity and alignment throughout its life cycle.

Hierarchy: The organizational structure with different levels of authority and responsibility. In the context of Guiding Star OKRs, it's about creating clarity and focus, not control.

Horizon: The time frame or future point in time that a goal or objective is aiming for. Guiding stars often have a longer horizon than traditional goals.

Incremental Delivery: An approach where work is delivered in small, viable increments, allowing for frequent feedback and adaptation—without the need for project milestones or tollgates.

Informal Networks: The web of relationships and connections between individuals within an organization, often based on trust and shared interests, which can facilitate knowledge sharing and collaboration.

Inspired Guiding Star: A goal that contributes in the same direction as a higher-level guiding star, ensuring strategic coherence across the organization. (This is not work breakdown or cascading goals.)

Intrinsic Motivation: The drive to engage in an activity for its inherent satisfaction or enjoyment, rather than for external rewards or pressures.

Iterative Process: A process that involves repeating cycles of planning, execution, and review, enabling continuous improvement and refinement.

Jobs-to-Be-Done (JTBD): A framework that focuses on understanding the underlying customer needs and the motivations behind their actions rather than just their demographic or behavioral attributes.

Key Results: The "KR" in OKRs—these are a quantitative and tangible way to track progress and understand what the objective will result in.

Last Responsible Moment: The concept of delaying decisions until the point where further delay would negatively impact the outcome, allowing for flexibility and adaptation.

Law of Mobility: A principle in Open Space Technology that encourages participants to move between discussions if they aren't learning or contributing, ensuring active engagement.

Lean Coffee: A structured, yet flexible, meeting format where participants collectively create and manage the agenda, fostering open discussion and knowledge sharing.

Local Guiding Star: A goal that's specific to a particular team or department and may not directly contribute to the overarching strategic direction.

Now-Next-Later Roadmap: A visual tool that categorizes initiatives into three time frames, providing a flexible and adaptable representation of the transformation journey.

OODA Loop: A decision-making cycle consisting of Observe, Orient, Decide, and Act, emphasizing the importance of rapid and continuous adaptation to changing circumstances.

Objectives: The "O" in OKRs—these are qualitative statements that describe the desired future state or outcome. They act as guiding principles for decision-making and inspire agile planning.

Open Space Technology (OST): A self-organizing meeting format that empowers participants to create and manage the agenda in real time, encouraging open dialogue and exploration of a central theme.

Opportunities and Outcomes (O&O) Artifact: A document capturing insights from product discovery, including customer needs, market trends, and technological advancements, which informs the selection of guiding stars.

Persistence: The ability to maintain focus and continue working towards long-term goals despite challenges and setbacks.

Plan-Do-Check-Act (PDCA) Cycle: An iterative process for continuous improvement, involving planning, implementing, evaluating, and adjusting actions based on feedback and learning.

Preserve Optionality: The strategy of delaying decisions until the last responsible moment, allowing for flexibility and adaptation as new information becomes available.

Product Discovery: The process of understanding customer needs, market trends, and technological possibilities to inform product development and innovation.

Pupation: The phase between strategy formulation and strategy execution, where guiding stars are integrated into agile planning, ensuring alignment between long-term goals and short-term actions.

Quenched Disorder: A state of productive chaos and unpredictability that fosters innovation and creativity, often arising from spontaneous interactions and diverse perspectives.

Raising the Horizon: The practice of extending the time frame or ambition of a guiding star when significant progress has been made or when a broader perspective is needed.

Refactoring (in OKRs): The process of improving the clarity and effectiveness of key results without altering the fundamental objective, ensuring better understanding and alignment.

Set-and-Forget: A common pitfall in strategic planning where goals are set but not actively monitored or adjusted, leading to misalignment, low engagement, and missed opportunities.

Sprint Goal: In Scrum, the overarching objective that a development team aims to achieve within a sprint or iteration, typically lasting one to two weeks.

Strategy: The overarching plan or direction to achieve a long-term goal or vision. See the sidebar, *What "Strategy" and "Execution" Mean in This Book.*

Strategy Broadcast: A company-wide communication event where the selected guiding star OKRs are shared, ensuring everyone understands and aligns with the strategic direction.

Strategy Execution: The process of putting the strategy into action. In the context of the Guiding Star OKR framework, it's influenced by the strategic direction set by the guiding stars. See the sidebar, *What "Strategy" and "Execution" Mean in This Book.*

Team of Teams: A network of interconnected teams and individuals who collaborate and share knowledge to achieve a common goal, transcending traditional organizational boundaries.

Timebox: A fixed period during which a specific set of tasks or activities are planned and executed.

Transformation "Whys": The clear and compelling reasons behind an organization's decision to adopt the Guiding Star OKR framework, often focused on overcoming specific challenges.

Transformation Lead: The individual or team responsible for guiding and facilitating the implementation of the Guiding Star OKR framework within an organization.

Transformation Roadmap: A visual representation of the planned steps and new practices involved in implementing the Guiding Star OKR framework, allowing for flexibility and adaptation.

Trifecta Challenge: The challenge of balancing persistence, alignment, and adaptability in pursuit of long-term goals, ensuring that none of these forces are stifled.

Unified Task List: A single list encompassing all tasks—both urgent and strategically important—ensuring long-term goals remain visible and prioritized alongside immediate demands.

Wardley Mapping: A visual tool used to analyze and understand a customer's value chain, highlighting the evolution and interdependencies of different components within their business.

Bibliography

[Bro95]   Frederick P. Brooks Jr. *The Mythical Man-Month: Essays on Software Engineering.* Addison-Wesley, Boston, MA, Anniversary, 1995.

[CD97]   Michael Cowley and Ellen Domb. *Beyond Strategic Vision: Effective Corporate Action with Hoshin Planning.* Routledge, London, UK, 1997.

[Chr16]   Clayton Christensen Taddy Hall Karen Dillon David Duncan. *Competing Against Luck: The Story of Innovation and Customer Choice.* Harper Business, New York, NY, 2016.

[Cor04]   Robert Coram. *Boyd: The Fighter Pilot Who Changed the Art of War.* Little, Brown and Company, New York, NY, 2004.

[de 85]   Edward de Bono. *Six Thinking Hats: An Essential Approach to Business Management.* Little, Brown and Company, New York, NY, 1985.

[Doe18]   John Doerr. *Measure What Matters: How Google, Bono, and the Gates Foundation Rock the World with OKRs.* Penguin, New York, NY, 2018.

[Dru54]   Peter Drucker. *The Practice of Management.* HarperCollins Publishers, New York, NY, 1954.

[GNP94]   Steven Goldman, Roger Nagel, and Kenneth Preiss. *Agile Competitors and Virtual Organizations: Strategies for Enriching the Customer.* Van Nostrand Reinhold, New York, NY, 1994, 2015, 1997, 1992, 2013.

[Har15]   Yuval N. Harari. *Sapiens: A Brief History of Humankind.* HarperCollins Publishers, New York, NY, 2015.

[Hor13]   Wim Hordijk. Autocatalytic Sets: From the Origin of Life to the Economy. *Bio Science.* 63[11]:877–881, 2013.

[Kah13]   Daniel Kahneman. *Thinking, Fast and Slow*. Farrar, Straus and Giroux, New York, NY, 2013.

[LM14]   Henri Lipmanowicz and Keith McCandless. *The Surprising Power of Liberating Structures: Simple Rules to Unleash A Culture of Innovation*. Liberating Structures Press, Seattle, WA, 2014.

[McC15]   Stanley McChrystal. *Team of Teams: New Rules of Engagement for a Complex World*. Portfolio, New York, NY, 2015.

[Owe97]   Harrison Owen. *Open Space Technology: A User's Guide*. Berrett-Koehler, San Francisco, CA, 1997.

[PP03]   Mary Poppendieck and Tom Poppendieck. *Lean Software Development: An Agile Toolkit for Software Development Managers*. Addison-Wesley, Boston, MA, 2003.

[Sie15]   Kathy Sierra. *Badass: Making Users Awesome*. O'Reilly Media, Inc., Sebastopol, CA, 2015.

[Ton03]   Joan Tonn. *Mary P. Follett: Creating Democracy, Transforming Management*. Yale University Press, New Haven, CT, 2003.

[Wal92]   Mitchell Waldrop. *Complexity: The Emerging Science at the Edge of Order And Chaos*. Simon and Schuster, New York, NY, 1992.

[Wat04]   Duncan J. Watts. *Six Degrees: The Science of a Connected Age*. W. W. Norton & Company, New York, NY, 2004.

Index

Thank you!

We hope you enjoyed this book and that you're already thinking about what you want to learn next. To help make that decision easier, we're offering you this gift.

Head on over to https://pragprog.com right now, and use the coupon code BUYANOTHER2025 to save 30% on your next ebook. Offer is void where prohibited or restricted. This offer does not apply to any edition of *The Pragmatic Programmer* ebook.

And if you'd like to share your own expertise with the world, why not propose a writing idea to us? After all, many of our best authors started off as our readers, just like you. With up to a 50% royalty, world-class editorial services, and a name you trust, there's nothing to lose. Visit https://pragprog.com/become-an-author/ today to learn more and to get started.

Thank you for your continued support. We hope to hear from you again soon!

The Pragmatic Bookshelf

SAVE 30%!
Use coupon code
BUYANOTHER2025

Agile Retrospectives, Second Edition

In an uncertain and complex world, learning is more important than ever before. In fact, it can be a competitive advantage. Teams and organizations that learn rapidly deliver greater customer value faster and more reliably. Furthermore, those teams are more engaged, more productive, and more satisfied. The most effective way to enable teams to learn is by holding regular retrospectives. Unfortunately, many teams only get shallow results from their retrospectives. This book is filled with practical advice, techniques, and real-life examples that will take retrospectives to the next level—whether your team is co-located, hybrid, or remote. This book will help team leads, scrum masters, and coaches engage their teams to learn, improve, and deliver greater results.

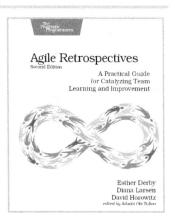

Esther Derby, Diana Larsen, David Horowitz
(298 pages) ISBN: 9798888650370. $53.95
https://pragprog.com/book/dlret2

Program Management for Open Source Projects

Every organization develops a bureaucracy, and open source projects are no exception. When your structure is intentional and serves the project, it can lead to a successful and predictable conclusion. But project management alone won't get you there. Take the next step to full program management. Become an expert at facilitating communication between teams, managing schedules and project lifecycle, coordinating a process for changes, and keeping meetings productive. Make decisions that get buy-in from all concerned. Learn how to guide your community-driven open source project with just the right amount of structure.

Ben Cotton
(190 pages) ISBN: 9781680509243. $35.95
https://pragprog.com/book/bcosp

Become an Effective Software Engineering Manager

Software startups make global headlines every day. As technology companies succeed and grow, so do their engineering departments. In your career, you'll may suddenly get the opportunity to lead teams: to become a manager. But this is often uncharted territory. How do you decide whether this career move is right for you? And if you do, what do you need to learn to succeed? Where do you start? How do you know that you're doing it right? What does "it" even mean? And isn't management a dirty word? This book will share the secrets you need to know to manage engineers successfully.

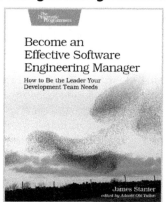

James Stanier
(396 pages) ISBN: 9781680507249. $45.95
https://pragprog.com/book/jsengman

The Stress Equation

Workplace stress is not the weakness of individuals; it's caused by systemic problems. Armed with the insights in this book, you can identify, analyze, and systematically reduce the factors that lead to poor health, low productivity, and personal burnout. This book gives you a framework for understanding stress, and a vocabulary to make it easier to discuss it among colleagues. Stress can be fixed; find out how.

Marcus Lagré
(126 pages) ISBN: 9798888651018. $35.95
https://pragprog.com/book/stresseq

Competing with Unicorns

Today's tech unicorns develop software differently. They've developed a way of working that lets them scale like an enterprise while working like a startup. These techniques can be learned. This book takes you behind the scenes and shows you how companies like Google, Facebook, and Spotify do it. Leverage their insights, so your teams can work better together, ship higher-quality product faster, innovate more quickly, and compete with the unicorns.

Jonathan Rasmusson
(138 pages) ISBN: 9781680507232. $26.95
https://pragprog.com/book/jragile

Software Estimation Without Guessing

Developers hate estimation, and most managers fear disappointment with the results, but there is hope for both. You'll have to give up some widely held misconceptions: let go of the notion that "an estimate is an estimate," and estimate for your particular need. Realize that estimates have a limited shelf-life, and re-estimate frequently as needed. When reality differs from your estimate, don't lament; mine that disappointment for the gold that can be the longer-term jackpot. We'll show you how.

George Dinwiddie
(246 pages) ISBN: 9781680506983. $29.95
https://pragprog.com/book/gdestimate

The Pragmatic Bookshelf

The Pragmatic Bookshelf features books written by professional developers for professional developers. The titles continue the well-known Pragmatic Programmer style and continue to garner awards and rave reviews. As development gets more and more difficult, the Pragmatic Programmers will be there with more titles and products to help you stay on top of your game.

Visit Us Online

This Book's Home Page
https://pragprog.com/book/snokrs
Source code from this book, errata, and other resources. Come give us feedback, too!

Keep Up-to-Date
https://pragprog.com
Join our announcement mailing list (low volume) or follow us on Twitter @pragprog for new titles, sales, coupons, hot tips, and more.

New and Noteworthy
https://pragprog.com/news
Check out the latest Pragmatic developments, new titles, and other offerings.

Save on the ebook

Save on the ebook versions of this title. Owning the paper version of this book entitles you to purchase the electronic versions at a terrific discount.

PDFs are great for carrying around on your laptop—they are hyperlinked, have color, and are fully searchable. Most titles are also available for the iPhone and iPod touch, Amazon Kindle, and other popular e-book readers.

Send a copy of your receipt to support@pragprog.com and we'll provide you with a discount coupon.

Contact Us

Online Orders:	*https://pragprog.com/catalog*
Customer Service:	*support@pragprog.com*
International Rights:	*translations@pragprog.com*
Academic Use:	*academic@pragprog.com*
Write for Us:	*http://write-for-us.pragprog.com*